PUTTING FEET ON THE TRIVIUM

Published by Logos Press
P.O. Box 8729, Moscow, ID 83843
800.488.2034 | www.logospressonline.com
Tom Garfield

Putting Feet on the Trivium: The Classical, Christian Administrator's Handbook

Cover and interior design by Samuel Dickison.

Printed in the United States of America.

PUTTING FEET ON THE TRIVIUM

THE CLASSICAL, CHRISTIAN ADMINISTRATOR'S HANDBOOK

By
Tom Garfield

CONTENTS

CHAPTER 11

APPENDICES

INTRODUCTION

The question I like to begin my administrative training courses with is always the same: "Why on earth would you want to be a Christian school administrator?" Now, lest you rush to judgement and misconstrue my purpose in asking, allow me to assure you—I love my job. But in many ways getting into it was like getting married, or even more appropriately, having kids. If someone had stopped you in the nick of time, so to speak, and somehow accurately and convincingly described the "nitty" and perhaps even the "gritty" sides of marriage and babies, you probably wouldn't have gotten involved with either one. Me neither. But we would have missed out on so many blessings and all that good life that outweighs the aforementioned nit and grit! (Then, too, running from God's will is always a bad idea, just ask Jonah.) However, God is sovereign and His will is always best. He also knows our frames and accordingly He doesn't reveal too much to us, lest we ask the mountains to fall on us in a vain attempt to escape our destiny. Praise His Name!

This is good work. But truly it is not for the faint-hearted. Even as I write this, I have just returned from carrying a bloody little person in my arms to her mom's car, which then sped off to the doctor's office. The small lass had fallen off a bar swing and done a face plant into gravel. She was a scarlet mess and her cries echoed through-out the school as she was brought into the office for tender ministrations. Lord willing, by next week she'll have a few stitches in her head and will be swinging again with the best of them.

No two days are exactly alike and rarely does an hour go by that the tasks don't fluctuate swiftly from the mundane to the bizarre. Prior to the playground accident, I was on the phone with a city official who has a beef with our parking configuration. Not long before that, I was discussing the merits of Homer's *Iliad* with a fifth grade teacher. This afternoon I will meet with a CPA who is going over our internal controls for our annual financial report. In the meantime, I hope to arrange for some pea-gravel to be put on the playground (over the existing larger gravel), in order to soften the falls of other vulnerable, but thankfully, resilient little people.

Such is the work. And I haven't even alluded to the really hard or fun parts. But since you're reading this you probably have work to get on with and if I am going to be of any help to you, I'd better explain how this necessarily brief handbook is to be taken.

WHY I HAVE ADDED TO THE ABUNDANCE OF BOOKS...

It has been my privilege to have administrated Logos School for over twenty years at this time. From my shaky first days to my shaky yesterday, I have been immensely blessed to see God's working in our little school. Through loads of experiences, encountering lots of wonderful (and a few irritating) people, and even in taking a number of classes, God has shown me a few things about this work. For His own purposes He has seen fit to put Logos in a certain national spotlight for a time and we have been able to pass on His blessings to others. I trust this is the case with the material contained herein, as well. There are many other fine books on administrating Christian schools, but not too many on dealing with the unique elements of trying to put together a classical, Christian school. Hence my efforts here. I have tried to include the practical aspects, along with some personal anecdotes from Logos School's history. I hope they help illuminate, or at least provide some entertaining relief from the practical stuff.

The chapters and their order have been arranged with the following assumptions:

- That you, the reader, have been hired relatively recently for this work,
- That this type of school is somewhat alien to your experience,
- That you need to plunge right into, or plan to continue, this work.

Thus I have tried to anticipate the order of concerns you will be faced with, as you probably don't have the luxury of a year or two to bone up on all you will need to know. Your school has either begun or is on the verge of beginning and you don't have many opportunities to ponder the deeper things of life at this point. (You will need to take the time to do that soon, so get some of the books I refer to in the bibliography and chip away at them.) In any case, look over the list of topics and use this handbook in the way you find most appropriate and may God bless you mightily in your labors in His kingdom.

DEDICATION

There is no possible way I could have survived, much less, enjoyed these many years at Logos without my covenantal sweetie, Julie, supporting and encouraging me. She is also to be credited with urging me often, but kindly, to crank this thing out. If you enjoy it, thank her, too. If you don't like it, don't tell either of us.

Doug Wilson, long-suffering friend and pastor, deserves to be noted as well. As you will observe in the first chapter, it was he who served as God's recruiter to enlist my services in this branch of the kingdom's work. Unlike the Navy recruiter I listened to many years ago, Doug was honest about admitting he didn't know what we were all getting into.

And this certainly has been more of an adventure than a job.

CHAPTER ONE

Your Qualifications

It wasn't the first time Doug Wilson had thrown me a curve ball. This time, unbeknownst to me, it was a radical, life-altering idea....

"I'd like you to consider heading up the Christian school we're starting next fall. You know, be its administrator or principal or whatever. What do you think? Of course you'd need to be interviewed by the board we have."

Doug stood there, looking at me with his you-see-this-is-a-really-great-idea-don't-you? look. We were conversing in Crossroads Bookstore, a Christian bookstore begun by his father, Jim, back in 1971. It was now late autumn of 1980. I was in the middle of my student teaching stint at the local public high school, as the final requirement for finishing my undergraduate degree at the University of Idaho, in Moscow. Student teaching in secondary art, to be precise. To date, my classroom experience had consisted of about four weeks of watching the high school art teacher conduct, what else, art classes. True, I had assisted some of the students in their clay and painting projects, so I was not utterly devoid of hands-on, meaningful student-teacher interaction.

Nevertheless, as I stood there on that fall day, watching Doug's sincere face and hearing his sincere tone, I had to pause. I should not dismiss his proposal out of hand. This was not an offer to take lightly. Some serious possibilities had to be faced: perhaps this was a vital ministry to which God was calling me, perhaps it would help change the lives of many children, perhaps it would lead to a life-long career, perhaps I could use my interest in art at the fledgling school to teach finger-painting! After considering none of the aforementioned possibilities, with perhaps the exception of the last one....

"You've got to be kidding?!", I finally blurted out, "I am graduating in December with a B.F.A., Doug! That's a Bachelor of Fine Arts degree, and it's in secondary art, for goodness sake. In spite of the ed courses I have taken, I couldn't write a lesson plan to save my life. My most profound and recent educational experience with young children was successfully changing my daughter's diaper. And you want me to consider being a principal of a Christian school?" I laughed in a rather derisive tone. Actually, it was a very derisive tone. Anyone else being laughed at like that, after a sincere offer, either would have been just plain hurt and offended, or would possibly have shoved a nearby Christian book on *Loving Unconditionally* into my laughing mouth. Not Doug.

"Well, why don't you and Julie think and pray about it, just the same. If you have any questions about what we're doing, you could ask me, or give Larry Lucas or Shirley Quist a call. They're on the board, too. See ya!"

And with that, if my memory serves, he smiled and exited the scene.

As I said, it wasn't the first time he'd done something like that to me. Only this time, the effect would indeed be far more long-lasting and life-altering.

Upon returning home to my wife, Julie, I recounted Doug's proposition, with a fresh burst of chortling. Julie, while not seeing it in exactly the same hilarious light I had, did express some profound amazement. I would like to think that she was amazed by the many unknowns of such an offer, and not by the possibility of Doug having a temporary loss of sanity.

In any case, by that time in our lives, both Julie and I had known Doug long enough to normally hold his judgment in high esteem. Julie had been born and raised in Moscow, where agriculture and the university employ the vast majority of Moscow's residents. In the summer following her graduation from high school, Julie met the Jim Wilson family, Doug being the eldest of four children.

Jim and his family had moved to Idaho to open a Christian bookstore near the campus of Washington State University in Pullman, Washington, Moscow's neighbor city eight miles to the west. Another bookstore, Crossroads, was begun in Moscow near the University of Idaho campus shortly afterwards. Jim had begun a similar college campus outreach bookstore in Ann Arbor, Michigan, three years before moving out to Idaho. (Ironic historical note: the Ann Arbor bookstore was named "Logos.") While in Michigan, the Wilsons attended the same church my family attended. Like Julie, I was born and raised in a "town and gown" setting, only it was about ten times the population of Moscow (with a vastly superior football team!). Eventually, I came to spend almost as much time at the Wilson's home in Ann Arbor as I did at mine. Mrs. Bessie Wilson was always gracious to the many visitors in their home, even me.

The Wilsons moved out to Idaho in 1971, a year before my high school graduation. In December of 1972, I enlisted in the Navy and, after some months of training, spent three and a half years aboard a ship romantically referred to as a fleet oiler. I stayed in touch with Doug and his younger brother Evan during my tour of duty and visited Moscow several times on leave.

Doug's tour ended in 1975 and he returned to Moscow where he, rather quickly in my opinion, got married to one Nancy Greensides. Evan and I got out a year later and also came to Moscow for schooling. And there, rather quickly in my opinion, I got married to one Julie Olsen in 1977. We attended the church Doug and another man led which met in various and sundry places, including the city park. (This was the seventies, you will note.) Eventually Doug became the main teacher, and we all rocked on each Sunday with our blue jeans and guitars. After a couple of years of wandering from place to place, the church finally found a steady home in Greene's Body and Paint Shop. You've never really worshiped until you've done it with a Rainier Beer truck in your "sanctuary."

But things were not all flowers and peace in our little fellowship. Doug and several other brothers with young families were meeting on the sly to discuss, among other items, the possibility of forming a Christian school, of all things! Being the visionary I was, I sensed right away this was a cause and mission with which I wanted absolutely no association. Weren't we weird enough already? A body shop for church! Why did we have to look for more ways to make the community think we Christians were strange? Couldn't we even send our kids to normal, public schools, without questioning everything? Apparently not, I lamented to Julie at the time. Doug was also meeting regularly with Larry Lucas, a C.P.A., and Shirley Quist, a local farmer's wife, both of whom attended our church.

Larry and Shirley were of a mind with Doug, in terms of the necessity of a establishing a non-denominational Christian school (at the time there were only two other private schools in Moscow, a Catholic school and a Seventh Day Adventist school). These three individuals, with the advice and support of a number of other area Christians, spent the majority of 1980 putting plans together. By fall they had completed a survey of a number of churches to determine the interest in a potential school. The results convinced them that there was indeed enough interest to move ahead. Although no other church actually wanted to be officially connected or financially supportive of a Christian school, a number of individual families stated their strong desire to see such a project become reality. The planners continued their work. Curriculum materials were to be obtained from a popular Christian textbook publisher. Based on the interest indicated in the surveys, the fledgling school board decided to "limit" enrollment to sixty students. Then, using a 15:1 student-teacher ratio, they planned to hire four teachers.

Now, in late 1980 the board began the search for the four staff members of the potential school. They would look for a facility later. Now was the time to seek those capable, loving, far-seeing individuals who would form the first staff of this little school. And like any solid, spiritually worthwhile missions effort, these staff members, like many missionaries before, would need very little in terms of money to sustain them. In fact, salaries, as such, were not part of the board's budget planning. Tuitions would only cover overhead costs. Teachers' pay? Well, that would come from the many gifts that would no doubt be poured out on such a project. In spite of such heady visions, the board rather quickly found two ladies willing to work under these conditions. And, to set possible snide suspicions aside, they were both capable, loving, and intelligent. The fact that they were also young and single may not have been a coincidence, either.

Thus it came to the point where Doug confronted me in Crossroads Bookstore with his wild proposition. After my easy brushing aside of such a hare-brained idea, I completed my student teaching at the local government high school. After sending out the requisite resumes, I received at least two art teaching job offers and did a lot of thinking and praying during the months of November and December of 1980. Prior to the idea, or more accurately, the seed of working at a Christian school had been planted in my mind, I probably would have jumped at either job offer. After all, it was what I had been trained for, or at least, it would keep food on the table for my young family. (Our first child, Carolyn, had been born in January of 1979, so there were three of us to think about.)

Now, with the public school job offers to consider, I paused and gave serious ruminations to that pesky idea of Doug's. Julie was no help at all in my relatively sudden uncertainty about my future vocation ... she just "trusted me to make the right decision." Great. I would like to say that I found a number of Scripture passages that guided me to make an inspired choice, but that's not the truth. It finally came down to just not having any rest or peace in my mind until I chased this idea down and stared it in the eye. So, after a fair bit of prayer, I met with Doug and asked to be interviewed by his school board.

As would be the requirement for all staff hirings in years to come, the board voted unanimously in its decision. Doug called to let me know they would like to offer me the job. If I accepted it, I would serve as principal and the fourth board member. God's timing is so good. By this point, I had been substitute teaching for the district for several weeks, after obtaining my degree and certificate. I didn't know much yet, but after working in a variety of public school classes, I knew that this was not what I wanted for a career. There had to be a better way to teach children and even enjoy doing it. Julie and I prayed again, and, gulping down the remainders of my foolish, pricked pride at being the only one to apply, I accepted the job offer. The first step into the immense gulf of the unknown began with a short "OK."

SO, WHAT'S YOUR STORY? WHAT QUALIFICATIONS DO YOU BRING TO THE JOB? SOME SOBERING THOUGHTS

The administrator is virtually the embodiment of being "all things to all people," or at least that often seems to be the expectation by those who employ you and the parents you will serve. Why do I say that?

Consider this:

You are responsible for everything—if anything goes wrong, you're responsible. Really. Even though you should learn to delegate to other qualified people, you retain responsibility to ensure all things are done well.

The character of the school program comes from the character of the administrator. Like ice cream, every school has a "flavor" of its own, i.e. the unique atmosphere, culture, student morale, congeniality of staff, programs, level of excellence, etc. The flavor will reflect what is important to you, the administrator. Are you Rocky Road, Bubblegum, Swirl, or just plain Vanilla? Whatever quirks, interests, strengths, weaknesses you have will show up and be amplified by the position you hold.

SOME BASIC QUALIFICATIONS TO CONSIDER FOR THE ADMINISTRATOR

What is your personality type? No one type is perfect, but if you're shy or easily depressed, it's going to be tough going for a while. A thick skin is absolutely imperative to have or be willing to develop. Are you drawn to children? Are they drawn to you? Can you speak confidently to all types and ages of people? Do you exude joy most often (not giddiness or fake smiles) so that people remark on your being "up" most of the time? Are you a better listener than a talker (a personal battle area)? Can you be serious without being depressing or boring? Can you have fun in the workplace? Do you have a fairly developed sense of humor? (You will certainly need it!) Does seeing the lights go on in students thrill you? Can you lead people and do they like to have you lead? These are just a few questions you should be able to answer clearly and honestly with large letters that spell Y-E-S, with the given that we all need grace, time and growth.

What outside interests/hobbies do you have? You should have some. They're fun to share with the kids, as appropriate. Kids love to discover that you have a "human" side. Your collections, hunting trophies, paintings, sports background, etc., all provide the students with insights into the adult world, yours in particular. It will increase their respect for you. For instance, I was bitten by the dramatic bug many years ago and pursuing it provides some very different activities than my day-to-day work. That in itself—doing something different for a while—can be as refreshing as rest. Not to mention (but I will), the very practical benefit of being able to act when needed in the workplace. Really. There are times when my heart has been practically broken by some news or a decision I had to make while at work, and yet, life had to go on. Little people expect you to be in control at all times and they need that security. So, whether it's a hobby or interest for you, you will find knowing how to act comes in handy.

The love of reading is a must, although time to do so is always hard to find, and will be more so, but keep working at it.

Are you a born organizer? That is, do you like ensuring that there is a place for everything and everything (normally) is in its place (or will go back there soon)? This is a must. Not a compulsive/obsessive type, just someone who enjoys places and programs being neat and orderly. Since you will have to insist on it, knowing how to organize and having an affinity for it will help. Besides, you will need to insist on organization from your entire staff; it should be obvious to all who know you that you are not a hypocrite on this point. Or any other, for that matter.

Do you find it easy to laugh? You don't have to be a stand-up comedian on the side, but you should be able to kid kids and be kidded (respectfully) by them. More importantly, your joy in the Lord should be evident in your frequent smile, laugh, and overall pleasant demeanor to all you meet. The kids love to share a joke or a laugh with you, and so do the parents, for that matter. Remember, the tone of the school, including the other staff members' relations, has a lot to do with your daily persona. Without a doubt, there will be tough times coming and being in the habit of looking for the lighter side of things will certainly help. Very honestly, there have been plenty of times where I have thought, and said, that we had a choice of either laughing or crying. There is a time for weeping, but the Scriptures seem to encourage a more joyful aspect, especially in tough times. I wish you could have met my father: he was the epitome of the above trait. All who met him loved being with him, and he was respected as much as he was liked.

Generally speaking, this is not work for an unmarried person. Ideally you should be joyfully married to a contented wife and, as God blesses, have some kids on whom you can practice what you preach. The benefits to understanding the critical nature of your work and being able to communicate it with great conviction are probably obvious. Yes, I did say "wife," because taking one thing with another, this is unequivocally a role best filled by a godly man. A lot could be said here in defense of that statement, but I will save it for later. For now, I am going to assume that you already have a good understanding of the leadership men are commanded to assume from a scriptural standpoint. Are there very capable women administrators? Of course. Frankly, if I had to list the best ones I have known, the list would be tilted to the female side. God gives many women superb administrative skills; that's why they run a home so well. Ability is NOT the issue—that's the red herring the world tosses out to us. Biblical qualifications for leadership should be implemented as soon as possible (since many schools seem to need/have a woman administrator to kick-start the work).

Your personal work ethics should be thought-out and ingrained. The old-fashioned, ever-appropriate Puritan work ethic should be part of your make-up. Do the "worst first." That is, tackle the tough jobs promptly, no procrastination. No clock-punchers or -watchers allowed. Mental, emotional, and even sometimes physical hard labor over frequently long hours is normal. But remember what I just said about biblical qualifications for leadership—doing a better job at school than at home with your own kids is a good way to bring God's curse on both places. Do right by your wife and kids first, then schedule time for work. Your board may need to be reminded of that priority order, too. If you need help at school, ask for it; don't burn the midnight oil except on rare occasions.

Honesty and integrity should be a given, although that requires a daily commitment to be a straight-shooter on your part; doing the right thing each time, no matter how inconvenient it may be. No problem, right? Right. That's why so many men have ruined their lives and, to the point, their schools. They compromised in the little things enough that great sin was just the next step. It's not inappropriate to very briefly mention here one of our greatest temptations as men, even boring, old, Christian administrators, i.e. women! You will likely be surrounded by women teachers and, if you get a high school, young ladies. They just might be attractive, too. Build physical and emotional safeguards around you, e.g. windows in your office door, standards for who you talk to and in what contexts. I trust you get the idea. Better and wiser men than I have written far more on this. (I recommend Doug Wilson's *Fidelity*.) Read them and be careful. Love your wife well and only, and you should be fine.

Don't look or live for "Atta-boy's!" Everyone enjoys recognition and praise for work well done. But if you have a hard time going without someone noticing and remarking positively ("Atta boy!") on your efforts frequently, this work is not for you. You will shrivel up like a tender flower lacking water. Your motivation and rewards should largely come from your inner satisfaction and the knowledge that this is where the Lord wants you and His pleasure is your encouragement. However, every once in a while, after a long day of dealing with many problems and concerns, someone, somewhere, may just step up to you and say in all sincerity, "I know it's late, but can you let Bernard into his classroom before you go home? He forgot his Latin workbook again!"

The spiritual qualifications for leadership in the church are very applicable to you. The qualifications Paul outlines for elders in I Timothy and Titus are rather appropriate for this work. With the exception of the qualification to be able to teach (as from the pulpit), the others are applicable to your calling in the school. Why shouldn't they be? You will be looked upon by the staff, students, and parents to fulfill that level of spiritual maturity. Would you want a lesser standard?

Knowing the Scriptures well is a must. This probably should go without saying, but a further point needs to be made. Considering the general malaise of Christian education today, it is imperative that as a classical administrator you should understand what a biblical worldview entails for your school and all its programs. That will take time, but the application of that worldview will necessitate your saturation in the Word. Not to mention the countless times, when you are dealing one-on-one with students, staff members, or parents, that your knowledge (and application) of Scripture will be heavily taxed. Daily time for refreshment in that knowledge, as our Lord well said, is part of your nutritional needs.

Your continuing sanctification should be apparent to you, your wife, and others. From what has been already said, particularly as noted in Paul's list, you should not be a new believer. Therefore, no matter how long you have been at the school, you should have been a Christian long enough that you can look back and see how God has been stripping away the layers, so to speak, that hinder your growth in Christ. Ask your wife and friends of a fair number of years. The fruit of good works and the Spirit should be obvious to them, at least. Your personal, moral "filters" should be getting better all the time, as they conform more and more to biblical reasoning and application. You should have a clear idea of being accountable—all the time, to God, your wife, your children, your church, etc.

Attending a convicting, worship-centered, God-fearing church is your lifeline. Put simply, you must be weekly worshiping in Spirit and in truth, and be challenged to think. Wanting to understand more of Him and how He would have you work in Him should almost make your head hurt. Is your church prodding you that way, or is it as compelling as tepid dishwater? You should find and contribute to good fellowship, but not rely on either the service nor the great folks for your keeping your spiritual barometer high (assuming that's a good thing). A personal note here regarding attending church: You will find, especially if you have families from your church attending your school, that you are viewed as being synonymous with your school. It took me a long time to figure out that I just had to deal with being "Mr. Logos", vs. Tom. Not that people actually called me that; it's just that when I talked to people, it seemed that's all we discussed. If it happens to you, relax. They still like you. Besides, it could be far worse—you might've been a CPA.

On a professional note, your degree of commitment is worth far more than any degree from college. That's not just a clever phrase (although I must admit it rolls off pretty well); it really is true. There is nothing wrong with having an administrative degree and/ or training, but the lack of it should not be a worry in itself. Of greater importance is having the attitude of a learner—a willingness to admit you have loads to learn, no matter what your background may be. With that kind of attitude you will approach your tasks as a seeker of information, rather than considering yourself a dispenser of profound wisdom. At the same time, it is in your best interest to have had some experience teaching others—young people, adults, dogs, whatever. Just having the personal opportunity of constructing instructional plans and seeing them through is a very worthwhile asset for your overseeing other teachers. You must be a life-long student yourself. Then, seek further, applicable training and it will be put to good use. As you get more familiar with your tasks, consider carefully your strengths and weaknesses. If, for instance, money management is a new or unfamiliar area for you, look into what the area colleges of business have to offer. Your board will be encouraged and pleased to see you taking the initiative to pursue more training and likely cover the costs. If that is not practical, consider just asking a fellow church member or school dad who is familiar with basic accounting procedures to give you some basics. Other classical, Christian administrators can be an excellent source of help, too. Finally, read lots of books—even books that kids in your school are reading.

Remember, God doesn't waste His time and training of His children—your prior jobs and experiences have been part of what has led you to this position. Even if the connections aren't obvious, you have been in training for this task all of your life, to this point. God will continue to hone your abilities as long as He wants you there.

You don't need to understand all the ramifications of a classical, Chris-

tian philosophy right away, but you should be buying and able to sell what you do know. It baffles my wee mind, but I have heard of administrators in classical schools who have their children elsewhere, even when the appropriate grades were offered in the school they were running. What is going on there? That's like walking into Wendy's and seeing the manager in a booth chowing down on a Big Mac! It's one of those things that cause you to say ... "Hmmm." To say the least, if you have school-age children, they should be in your school. This also has the benefit of giving you more eyes and ears to understand what is happening, practically and philosophically, in your school. (Note: Always keep in mind that children and wives see things from one perspective—theirs. You need to ALWAYS follow the biblical admonition to hear both sides first before rendering a judgment.)

In addition to showing your commitment to the school, and getting more first-hand input from the classrooms, a third benefit is that you will grow in your understanding of how this whole thing affects real children as they grow. That's philosophy with handles. It has been my privilege to be asked to speak at various locations around the nation about the benefits of classical education. The groups of people and their purposes, as well as their geography, differed a fair bit. But one thing they always had in common—they loved their children and wondered what this "classical thing" was going to do for their kids. Because I have had four children go through Logos, I always mention the benefit their education has been to them and the blessings my wife and I have enjoyed as a result. Wherever I am, that rings a bell every time.

Obviously that accumulation of experience with your own children takes years. In the meantime, then, you need to be reading and applying what you read as appropriate. I have included a recommended book list in the appendices. Now listen, if you're like me, you may be tempted to look at suggested reading lists the way you would a video rental agreement; that is, a quick scan for where to sign as you're on your way out. They could be stating in legalese that by your signature below you are selling your children into slavery, but because it's buried in a paragraph of eight-point font, you signed it anyway. Don't do that with the list I am giving you—read the books!

SOME HIGH PRIORITY STANDARD OPERATING PROCEDURES: (SOP)

This refers to the very basic, foundational, day-to-day hallmarks of your administrative style. We'll go into more specifics later. There is always room for personal style, and that will quickly become apparent to your parents and staff, especially if you are taking the helm from a previous administrator. But the following few SOPs are those I have found indispensable. There are probably more but these came to mind rather easily and are the ones I share most often in training seminars for administrators. You can see what you think after you try them:

The Open Door Policy

When I was in the Navy, we had a captain take over command of our ship for a time who actually said he believed in an "open-door" policy toward his men. We hadn't heard anything that funny since listening to our recruiters. We were to just stop on by and ... oh boy, this was a hoot, just talk to him! Yeah, right. And the pharaoh would have been happy to sit down and discuss brick-making problems with any of the Israelite slaves, too. Not likely. But administrators should be far more approachable than captains and pharaohs. So how does that practically work in a school setting? What it means is that virtually any time they want to, a student, parent, or staff member can knock on your office door and come in. They do not necessarily need an appointment or to have a certain social standing to come into your presence. Of course, they should bring some token or gift and approach you on their knees, but that's a given. Okay, never mind that last part. Generally the impression you want to convey is that nothing on your desk or computer is more important than the people you serve. And you need to practice your servanthood wherever possible.

Having said that, there are (of course) limits on this SOP. First of all, notice the categories of people above: students, staff, and parents. They should receive almost instant access, barring you being in a meeting already. Of secondary status would be community members of various sorts: businessmen, college professors (we have the University of

Idaho as a neighbor), mayors, building inspectors (they think they are pharaohs), etc. Way, way down the list of semi-welcomed types are the salesmen. But you still need to be polite. If you haven't asked them to come, greet them in the outer office and in a nice way let them know you're busy. For instance, out here, carrying a running chainsaw works well. Your secretary can be trained to spot the ones who get the "sorry, he's not available now" answers.

Another qualifier on this SOP is the topic of discussion at hand. If a student or parent or staff member has a concern, make sure the principles of Matthew 18 have been applied, i.e. have they gone first to the appropriate person or people? This is most applicable to parents (usually moms) who have a concern about a teacher. Remember, gossip is the no. 1 indoor sport of Christian schools, it seems. You get the idea. Be approachable, but be wise in how you process the query: Listen well, don't commit to any course of action without due thought (boy, is that good counsel!), be gracious, and take notes as needed. (See the next item.) Then, (practice saying this in front of a mirror) reply with: "Thanks. Let me do some thinking and praying about that and I will get back to you." Obviously, you better do that, too.

Put It In Writing!

This falls in the same line of thinking as one of my favorite little ditties—"Do it when you think of it!" Obviously it is impossible to do everything you would like or need to do exactly when you think of it, especially if you remember it in the middle of the night or during a worship service. For instance, since our church currently meets in our gym, it is extremely difficult for me to not look around during the sermon and see a zillion things I would like to address in the facility. Rather than sit and stew about all those things that need doing, or worse, fretting about forgetting them by the next day, I make a short note in my Day-Timer notebook. Then I can get back to focusing on the sermon. So, perhaps a workable modification and synthesis of the two ideas would be—"IF you can possibly do so, write it down when you think of it." People will make all sorts of requests and demands of you at all hours of the day. If you are at your desk and can act on a modest request right away, such as calling in the S.W.A.T. team, go ahead. My staff has worked with me long enough to know that if they stop me in the hallway and want me to remember what they say, they better also make a note to put in my mailbox. Go ahead; don't be afraid to admit your mind isn't a steel trap. Ask people to put it in writing for you if they really want you to act on their topic.

Obviously you should have some personal planner (I strongly suggest a Day-Timer) in which to jot your own plans and ideas. Then refer to your notes frequently and you just might get some work done. Or at least you'll know what you didn't accomplish that day.

Get To Know the Kids and Their Parents ASAP

The kids are always surprised at the beginning of the year when I call them by name. Perhaps they think someone with my chronological impairment would be lucky to correctly identify a stop sign. So they are amazed when I nail one name after another. My favorite image in this regard is in the original movie (with Peter O'Toole) of "Goodbye, Mr. Chips!" In the opening sequence, the ancient Chips stands in the main hall of the picturesque English school, greeting boy after boy by name as they pass by. That's what I want to do, too, especially if I could also have that great picturesque school!

Unfortunately I am a long way from either having Chips's ability or his school. I am more of a visual type, I remember faces easier than names. Therefore, I try to link something about each new child's appearance to his name. With enough concentration and by ensuring I greet them frequently in the first days of the new school year, I can pretty quickly identify the new students. (The returning students I already know, so all my efforts can be focused on just the new students.) Even the youngest ones will realize you love them when you quickly learn and use their names. A practical hint: After you have school photos taken (as soon as possible after school's back in session), and you get those strips of small file photos, have your secretary make class composites for you. The kids' names should already be on the photo. Keep studying the photos until you are confident you can ID any child in the hallways.

The parents are much harder to get to know by name. The dads especially are tough because they don't frequent the school as often as the moms. One administrator I know takes a family photo whenever a family is admitted to his school and then he posts it where he can see the picture frequently. I keep the school directory very handy so I can grab it while on the phone or when I see a parent in the auditorium. Since I know the child they are with, I can usually quickly look up the parents' names and use them confidently as I greet them. Given enough times like that, the names go into long-term memory eventually. Whatever it takes, show your love and interest in the students to get to know them ALL as soon as you can humanly do so.

Never Know Anything That the Parents Don't Know

Allow me to elucidate. Obviously you will and, frankly, should know more about how to educate the children than the parents do. That's why they hired you—"you" in a collective sense. What I mean by the above guideline is you shouldn't ever have some knowledge about a young person that the parents may not know, but should. This is particularly true when it comes to relationships at the secondary level. You will, if you're doing your job keeping your eyes and ears open, see and hear things the parents won't because they are not at the school. You will possibly even have students confide in you about how they feel toward another student. Just like adults, these young people can have their feelings hurt by others, motives and looks can be wrongly interpreted and resentments can easily develop, all without flaring up into a public conflagration.

When I become aware of these issues, I have to decide how to deal with that knowledge. What I tell the students is just what I said above—I can't know something, at least for very long, that their parents don't know. So, I give them a chance to tell their folks, say, within 24 hours. Then I will call. And a number of times I have had to let a dad know that he should have a talk with his child about such and such. Or that he should talk to another dad about the problems between their daughters (yes, that is usually the gender involved in such things).

There is also the strong possibility that you may see and/or hear about a "romantic" connection developing between two students, that is, if you have almost any number of students older than twelve. If you have your own children in the school, they will become additional eyes and ears for you on this topic, even without your asking (which you really shouldn't). Or, as has happened to me more than once, you may be confided to by one or more of the star-crossed lovers. Here again, whether I just observe it or actually get a first-hand account, I need to let the parents know about it, soon. I like to give the student the opportunity and time to do so first, then I call to ensure that message was accurate.

Here's the kick, though. Even though I will continue to do this and advocate that others (like you) follow suit, I won't guarantee the parental response will be positive. To be honest, I'd say, particularly when it came to the romantic situations, that my popularity rating has sometimes gone up and sometimes it's gone down, when I have informed the parents. About 50/50 overall, it seems. Some parents are very grateful and thank me for letting them know so they can give wise counsel to their progeny. Other parents have let me know that, essentially, they are aware of the situation and maybe I shouldn't be so suspicious of their child's intentions and/or that they have no problem with the young couple. "What's so wrong with an innocent high school crush, anyway?"

Sigh. Okay, chalk it up to their having the authority and not you.

However, should it slop over into your "turf," that is, become or continue to be obvious and distracting within the school environment, then by all means, exercise YOUR corporate authority and tell them to knock it off or suffer the consequences!

You're the Administrator, But Be a Visionary, Too

You have probably discovered that your board is largely made up of people who have a passion for having a "classical" school, whatever that means. As their zeal gains knowledge, their commitment to have the best classical school will grow. They will generate lots of ideas. That's all good. Most board members will have no idea how their vision will actually play out in the classrooms, but will try to come up with practical methods and ideas anyway. That's not so good. We will look at the board more closely later on, but for now suffice it to say that most board members are visionaries, not administrators. That's where you come in. You need to respectfully hear their ideas and then try to put feet on them.

The respect part is important, since you may be tempted, after you get to know the school's staff and operations better, to come unglued when a board member throws out a class-F, bone-headed idea. Relax. If you do what you should day after day, you will gain the confidence of the board, and they will naturally ask for your input before implementing most bone-headed ideas. Don't become known as a nay-sayer, i.e. someone who objects to anything new or different just because it may be a change or a challenge. God has placed those people on your board for a reason—they just might have some good ideas you need to consider.

For your part, though your strengths are and should be in the administrative area, you should also be constantly, critically examining the school for ways to improve it in any way possible. The better you get to know what is possible, through knowing what's happening in your classrooms, as well as looking at other classical schools' programs, you should become downright antsy to go further up and further in (as they say in Narnia). The fire in your belly should be stoked by each successful program your school implements. "How can we do this better next time? What other things like this can we be doing?" Not more things to do, doing things better! The popular syndrome called "burn-out" comes largely from boredom and weariness. I don't believe this should or has to happen to Christian workers. Look around, ask for ideas from your staff. Certainly before you take any prime cut ideas of your own to the board, get your staff 's input. Just as you like to give your input to the board before some things are put in place, your teachers may want to have a chance to modify your possibly bone-headed plans. Some fires need to be damped down a bit before people get burned.

My favorite analogy in considering our work is the image of a lighthouse keeper. I love lighthouses, so that may be a reason. Consider the work of those men, now long gone, replaced by electricity. Their primary job was to keep that very critically placed light burning brightly as a beacon of safety and information to the ships at sea. But the maintenance work was very hard and quite boring. Several times every day they had to fill and haul buckets of oil, which could weigh up to twenty-five pounds, up the dozens and dozens of winding steps to the top of the round tower. There they also had to constantly polish the brass, clean the cut glass and mirrors of the light. Every so often they even had to risk life and limb to paint those wonderfully designed towers. We administrators may not have lit the light, i.e. our school's founding philosophical vision, but we must maintain it. To do that we must understand its critical nature and be willing to labor day in and day out to make sure it burns brightly for all to see. Hope that helps you picture your work a bit better, too.

CHAPTER TWO

Planning for Opening Day

Our first child, Carolyn, had turned two by the time I accepted the job at Logos. Being a quick learner, Carolyn was also working on driving her mother and me nuts by singing the alphabet song repeatedly. She needed some steadying influence. How about another sibling in the home? Along about February we discovered that a small bundle of steadying influence would be arriving in October. So, while I continued subbing in the Moscow public schools and planning for the new Christian school, Julie worked on preparing our apartment for another small tenant.

While I often imagined Carolyn eventually attending the school we were planning, another little girl had the distinction of being much of the primary impetus for the school's creation. Doug and Nancy Wilson's oldest daughter, Bekah, was going to be kindergarten age by the time we opened the school's doors. It was no coincidence—her parents had been praying and planning for the school with her in mind.

As the spring of 1981 progressed, the board and staff (still lacking one teacher) met quite a few times to discuss plans and look at curriculum ideas. It was decided that a public informational meeting, both to disseminate information about the school and possibly garner interest, would be planned for March. We held it in a local restaurant's banquet room and about thirty people showed up. Our board chairman, Larry Lucas, did an admirable job of outlining the mission and purpose of the proposed non-denominational, Christian school. However, opening ourselves up for questions may have been a mistake. We were handling them pretty well until someone asked where the school would call home.

"Well, we're still looking for a place. We are sure open to suggestions," Larry answered hopefully. Meaningful looks were lobbed back and forth between the attendees. But, overall, the evening was a modest success, with a couple of families expressing interest in enrolling their little ones.

Where to have the school? It couldn't be avoided any longer. We hadn't exactly been avoiding the need, but with summer coming on, the issue moved to front burner status. Knocking on several church's doors produced no offers, not even the suggestion of a stable out back. Creative ideas were thrown on the table. A helpful realtor even showed us a couple of houses "that might work for you, at least to get started." However, even with only sixteen students, we would need a pretty good-sized house. "Cheaper by the dozen" was certainly not the story for us.

Other work went on in between searching for a facility. We decided to go with the most popular Christian school materials publisher to supply our curriculum needs. By June, some of the ordered materials had arrived and we scrutinized them with all the excitement and keen insight of a teenager buying his first used car. Gee, they were colorful, and there were posters and everything! At that point in time, we had just about as much discernment as Alice in Wonderland, trying to choose the wisest course to take in a very unfamiliar landscape and swallowing a lot of weird stuff.

Finally, thank God!, in late June a wonderful group of Christian folks at the Paradise Hills Church of God came through for us. They offered to let us finish their basement with funds they would borrow from their church district. We would repay their loan through our rent. The small congregation had huge hearts and a large building they had built themselves. The unfinished basement area was big enough to house several classrooms. For our first year we decided to construct three classrooms, one each for kindergarten, lower elementary, and upper elementary. We also planned two bathrooms and a school office. That took up about half of the unfinished basement area.

They would allow us to use their sanctuary for assemblies and their fellowship hall for indoor PE, lunch, and other fun events. What a real blessing! Much better than that split-level house or even the large barn we had considered briefly. Plans and construction moved into high gear.

However, while that problem was being solved, another very serious one was developing in our home. Julie was only about five-and-a-half months pregnant but she began to have contractions. She was put into the Pullman hospital (about eight miles west of Moscow). In March I had begun a bread-on-the-table job at Skipper's restaurant and now, without Julie at home, I had to care for Carolyn alone. Christian friends watched her when I went to work, but leaving her weeping day after day at other homes indelibly burned itself on my heart.

Time in the hospital didn't seem to be stabilizing things much for Julie. Even so, when the crisis came on July 14, it was a real surprise. On that warm, sunny morning I had left Carolyn with our next-door neighbor. Before going to work, I showed the new school facility to our final teacher to be hired for the year. She would have the first and second graders in a mixed level class. After comparing notes with her for preparations for her class, I left the church and arrived at Skipper's only to be told that I was needed at home, pronto. But by the time I got home, my neighbor informed me that they'd taken Julie to Deaconess Hospital in Spokane by ambulance.

Taking time only to kiss Carolyn and call my sister Judy to accompany me, I cruised as fast as I lawfully could (and a little more) to Spokane, eighty miles to the north. After an anxious trip, we arrived at the wrong hospital. We were given directions and once there we were informed Julie was on the third floor, Obstetrics and Maternity. We were met by a nurse who let us know Julie was just about to go into surgery to deliver the baby. Or, as the matronly nurse who met us put it, "It's about time someone got here for that poor gal!"

For awhile things were on fast-forward, it seemed to me. I remember putting on the paper clothes that doctors wear and being told to "Stand there.", near Julie's head. Intense lights, mumbling and softly shifting people in green, rustling outfits. Low hums, clinks. More mumbling, higher pitched.

Prayer came easily: "Father, please just get us through this. Help Julie."

"Mr. Garfield?", a green person said over the hum and mumbles. I looked up to see a doctor holding a gangly, red little body about a foot long. "You have a son, Mr. Garfield." I had honestly momentarily forgotten about the fact that a baby was also involved in this whole operation.

After allowing me a brief glance at our very little boy, they whisked him into a wheeled isolet (a special incubator) and told me I could check on him later in the N.I.C.U. (Neonatal Intensive Care Unit), a place Julie and I would learn to love and loathe in months to come. The rest of the day was spent tending Julie, calling our moms, listening to them cry, and, finally being able to see Seth Thomas. After weaving among several other aquarium-like isolets, I found Seth. On the card under his name was written, "2 lbs., 3 oz.". He lay, red as a sausage, under more lights, wires sprouting from him like the back of a stereo. I measured the size of his hand from finger-tip to wrist by comparing it to my fingers. His whole hand was the size of the last knuckle on my thumb. My son ... born three months early. What a guy!

Then the days and weeks of being separated as Julie stayed in Spokane with mutual friends of Shirley Quist's. Days and weeks of three steps forward and two back, as we prayed and willed Seth to grow stronger. Two and a half months would go by before, handling him like a Delft plate, we were able take him home.

One day, as we knew it would, the hospital's business office asked to meet with us to discuss our somewhat sizable tab. The woman we met with was extremely nice and understanding, even when we let the cat out of the bag and told her that not only did we not have insurance, but that I would not actually be paid a salary in my new school job.

"You d-don't know what you will make each month?"

"Nope. See, it's sort of like mission work. You know, where we'll receive gifts, as they come in."

Nodding as though this was the most reasonable idea she'd ever heard, she asked us what we could commit to as a regular payment. Seeing as how we were in the process of wracking up a hospital bill equivalent to the sticker price of a modest new house, I threw out a figure I hoped wouldn't sound too ridiculous, considering everything. She accepted it right off and drew up the forms. Julie and I looked at each other, both with one thought—"How in the world will we pay what we've just committed to?"

A special note of profound thanks to our parents needs to be interjected here. Both sets would have been perfectly justified in telling us that, in light of our current situation, going ahead with the new school job would be like putting our life's savings into eight-track players. That's putting it very mildly—they would have been justified in telling me to get a "real" job! And they would have been echoing my own thoughts and fears. But they didn't say anything like that, instead they just poured loads of love and support into us as we waited and prayed day after day.

Was this whole episode with Seth a test of our faith, or even just our vision for the ministry we were entering? I honestly don't know, and would not presume to know my Father's mind. We were set on a course and to veer from it never seemed to be a viable option. Seth did grow and much more happened to him and us during that tense time than I can relate here. Suffice it to say that I do know that the timing of Seth's homecoming—just days before the school opened—was a tangible blessing to me. Knowing he was home made both Julie's and my burden lighter. Seeing what it can take to get a little baby safely into the world also taught me how precious each child is; I would have a hard time taking a child for granted after this.

A final note about that trying period of our lives: our dear Father truly put a hedge of protection from fear around our hearts. I always expected Seth to live. I honestly never doubted that he would. Only later, much later, did I find out he had had a one-in-three "chance" of living. Such is the Holy One's sovereignty and kindness.

During the time Seth was in Spokane, a school family and staff barbecue was held in August. We cooked the obligatory burgers and dogs, watching our charges-to-be charging around the backyard of Jim and

Bessie Wilson's home. The fledgling teachers and administration were wondering how all this was going to work, but the kids had no problem figuring it out. They quickly discovered who was in who's class and shared the joy and excitement of meeting new friends. After the meal, I called all the families together, and we had the kids group up by grades, with the appropriate teacher. They looked more like teams for kick-the-can than classes of school children, but the kids thought it was neat. I still marvel at the faith and trust of the parents gathered there. Competence and professionalism did not exactly describe the teachers and administration present. Especially the administration, dressed in the ever-present jeans. Yet, to my knowledge, none of the parents backed out that night. Rather they made all the staff feel appreciated and supported.

As the summer of '81 ended, my new son and the new school were both off to a somewhat shaky start.

And, also with both, only God could bring growth and stability.

WHAT PLANS HAVE BEEN LAID FOR YOUR SCHOOL?

Not every administrator has the privilege and opportunity to be in on the "ground floor" of planning the school. Regardless, there are some primary areas of consideration that you need to examine, whether you have been there since Day One or not. If your board has already thoroughly thought these issues through and the school has been clicking along smoothly—great! Then you need to become familiar with them; after all, you're the one who is responsible for making them happen now. On the other hand, perhaps there are a few topics the board, in its initial zeal, may not have considered and you will therefore need to address. So, what are they? In a rough form, here are some of the big-picture essentials:

Philosophy of education

I trust it's not a big surprise to you to discover that this would be the all-encompassing, highest priority, the big "E" on the chart. What are your (collective) basic beliefs about education? Who has been given authority to do it? What does God say about it? How does your philosophy answer and counter the our culture's "secular" approach? You get the idea: There should be a documented vision and philosophy statement for the school that your board has adopted, even if they didn't create it. I will also assume you want a classical and Christian approach to education (otherwise why are you reading this?). The important point here is that you know, can articulate, and have documented WHY you desire this philosophy of education. If, for some reason, you are still not as clear on the 'whats' of classical, Christian education, I would direct you to the Resources Appendix at the end of this handbook. Far better brains than mine have done a good job of explaining this type of education, and in formats you can easily share with your board and staff.

There are a few other overall considerations related to your educational philosophy:

- Governmentally, will your school be church-run? Family-run (as in a co-op)? Board-run? Why did the school choose the option they have in place? The reasons should be documented, based on the philosophy.
- What, if any, affiliations with state, local district, other educational organizations—e.g. A.C.C.S., A.C.S.I., etc., will you have? What is your stance on vouchers, tax credits, etc.? (Quick answer—avoid governmental entanglements like the plague!)
- Where will you turn for answers to philosophical questions?

If you are part of an existing Christian school that is changing over to a classical approach, you'll have a whole shipload of issues to deal with in the philosophical realm. For instance, is this change conducive to or in conflict with the current teaching structure? Philosophy issues and differences could easily become a battleground for personalities when significant changes are contemplated. Beware.

School program structure (not the facility)

These choices will have a tremendous, practical affect on implementing your vision:

- Will you have K-6?, K-8?, P-6?, 1-6?, just 7-12?, 7-9?, 9 -12?, K-12?, P-12?, Day care program included? (A word on daycare programs—Don't! The money isn't worth the compromise with biblical family principles.)
- What will the classroom structures be like? Student to teacher ratio? Combination classes (mixing more than one grade in a classroom)? Low ratios are nice, but financially difficult, especially when you are just starting. Combo classes are a way to get the best from your staff and allow more students in the school. Consider them only for short-term, though. It is a difficult task in the best of situations. And don't even think of combining more than three grades (two is more workable) unless you want to see a teacher spontaneously combust.

What are the set and understood lines of authority within the school? A board of some sort is desirable; a one-man show is not. Where do you fit in? Under the board, above the rest of the staff is the norm. For seven years I was on the board as well as being the head administrator. I would strongly recommend against this! It is too hard to wear both hats and switch them, especially when you failed to convince the rest of the board and must submit as the administrator. More on this later.

Has the necessary documentation been put together? Do you have a job description? A sample is in the resources appendix.

A Sample Checklist for First Day Preparations

Here is a simple list of considerations that may fit your situation as you prepare for the opening day (most of which I didn't do the first year!):

JULY

- Recheck, revise adopted annual budget (enrollments, payroll), tell board
- Complete all textbook, materials purchases
- Confirm, begin addressing facility needs: maintenance, improvements, new furniture, classroom needs

- Address any staffing needs, ensure all work agreements (contracts) are current
- Update policy manual (check with board clerk)
- Update, revise staff manuals, student-parent handbooks—send new handbook to ALL families
- Finalize yearly calendar, mail out
- Mailing to families/staff to give updates on new students, staff members, policies, programs, events, supplies lists, etc.
- Continue advertising for and interviewing new families.

AUGUST

- Compare adopted budget to current payroll, expenses to date, enrollment, needs expected; adjust as necessary
- Plan for/execute teacher orientation—inventory sheets, staff manuals, schedules (daily, recess, etc.), updated curriculum guides, etc. (See more on this under Programs)
- Determine all last orders, confirm status on all outstanding materials orders
- Determine unforeseen classrooms needs (after staff returns late in month)
- Prepare all family-related documents, e.g. field trip permission, emergency notification, etc. include letter detailing start of school plans, mail out
- Receive, store all class supplies, texts, books
- Determine final enrollment, classroom needs for students
- Develop Administrative goals for the year, get board approval, pass on to other staff
- Ascertain all staff have work agreements, other necessary documents, e.g. tax forms
- Equip all staff with needed manuals, esp. curriculum guides
- Acquaint staff with new/revised policies from board

- Prepare, distribute, and collect current inventories of texts/ materials
- Finalize all student, staffing needs

OUR GRAND OPENING

Oh, mercy! It would have to be on the third floor! Sigh. Oh, well. It was the only piano we had seen, so I bid on it. The other auction attenders, being smarter than I was, allowed me to gain the top bid rather easily. In fact, no one else bid. ("Check out the idiot bidding on a piano on the third floor! Snort, guffaw!") "Sold! To the guy about to get a hernia!" Eruption of general laughter among the auction attendees, with the exclusion of one.

The piano wasn't the only thing we bought that day, but it was the most memorable. Shirley Quist, Larry Lucas, and I had driven to Spokane in early August, 1981, to get some used school furniture at the public school auction. Over many years to come, I would be able to obtain the vast majority of our school's furniture by taking advantage of the Spokane district's use-it-or-lose-it budgeting policy. We saved literally tens of thousands of dollars buying used furniture with years of life left in it.

This particular auction was an all-day affair due to the tremendous amount of stock to auction off. We had all been astounded at the huge warehouse rooms stacked with desks, chairs, bookshelves, kitchen equipment, lab supplies, and shop tools, just to mention a few specifics. Table tops were covered with odd bits and pieces of electronic equipment, maps, art supplies, P.E. items, and other identifiable and unidentifiable gee-gaws. We had brought a shopping list and tried very hard to stick to it. But we couldn't get through any room without at least one of us saying, "Hey! Check this out! Won't we need one of these, sometime?" And, depending on how convincing the person's reasons were, we would either bid on it, or just say, "Well, let's see how much it goes for...."

We were able to purchase enough chairs, desks, blackboards and one piano, among other miscellaneous, "neat" stuff, to outfit our little school. We loaded the Quist's grain truck, drove back to Moscow, unloaded the furniture, and surveyed the overall readiness of the school. In just a few weeks the school doors would open for the first time. The walls for the three classrooms were ready for paint. The bathrooms still needed the fixtures installed, but the plumbing contractors were great guys and we knew we could count on them. (In fact, they were Christians and would be of incalculable support to the school in years to come.) The carpeting would be laid after the painting was done. I looked into "my" office; a ten-by-twelve foot room that would house the secretary's desk, my desk, and some teacher-work area, i.e. the duplicating machine. (A photocopier was a far-off dream at that time.) It all looked wonderful!

The basement level wing of the church had windows facing east and a door to the outside play area. The school would be located in the northern half of the wing, closest to the stairs and fellowship hall. The unfinished, southern half of the same wing would provide future expansion possibilities. For now, it contained church storage and a sizable population of mice.

After the others left, I went outside to cool off from the long, hot day of work. The grassy play area that would be the playground for the kids was a relatively narrow piece of ground that quickly dropped off to a steep, weed-covered slope of about a hundred yards. At the bottom of this hill was a farmer's field of about fifteen acres.

From the top of the hill behind the church, you could see much of the north and east views of Moscow. It really was a beautiful view. From my office window the Moscow "mountains", a long, undulating ridge of hills about a thousand feet high, could be easily seen. While in the Navy I came to love the ocean's ability to shift and change its colors and texture daily. The mountains were like that too, their colors and shadows never looked the same two days running. The green and blue hues would shift constantly, according to the each day's light. The highest tree tops would get the first frosty dusting of snow in the winter, letting us know winter was coming. In the spring, the hillsides would be a rich aquamarine, the forest of firs looking bushier, somehow, than they had in the winter.

But that day I wasn't thinking about how the mountains would look year after year. I was thinking about how small the grassy play area was, and the fact that there wasn't one thing for the kids to play with or climb on. We had spent many hours preparing the inside of the school, but the outside would have to wait until after school began, there just wasn't time to do it all. The weedy, wide slope of the hill on which the church sat would provide some diversion, as it turned out. The boys especially would find it of great interest. Again, though, I was spared any foreboding; ignorance can be bliss, for a while.

The last few weeks of preparation were a strange mix of time perceptions for me: the days weren't long enough in readying the school, and yet they weren't short enough as I monitored, long-distance, Seth's progress in the hospital. The schoolwork was definitely therapeutic, though. It displaced, for a while, my anxiety about Seth still struggling in the hospital eighty miles away. Along with the teachers, I immersed myself in moving furniture to the rooms, watching the carpet being laid, carrying in far more books than I could imagine seventeen students needing, and painting, painting, and more painting. As August's last days ticked off, the teachers feverishly put lesson plans together (based on absolutely no guidance from me or any other clear directives), and decorated their walls with those colorful posters. I worked on the office—adjusting my desktop items, determining which side was best for my phone, trying out my chair, and generally trying to figure what in the world I was going to do once the kids got there. Oh yes, I also obtained a nice, tall bookshelf from a generous family. Of course, then I had to find some intellectual-looking books to put on it. Nothing is so naked as an empty bookshelf. Perhaps some well-placed models would suffice? Ah, yes. Work, work, work.

We had set the Tuesday after Labor Day in early September as the grand opening date. As with many such incidental decisions, this too would become a TRADITION. None of the staff spent much time away from the school that holiday weekend. Quite a few school families also spent their Labor Day helping to clean, organize, and generally make the school look more like a school than a done-over basement. And, by George, it really did look a bit like a school! From the carpeted hallways, to the neat rows of desks in the three classrooms, each with an orderly pile of books on top ... the place just might pass for a school. A very small one, but a school nonetheless. I counted the desks in each room for the zillionth time; six in the kindergarten, eight in the combination first/second grade room, and three (one each for our token fifth, sixth, and ninth graders) in the corner room.

Monday, Labor Day, came to a close. It was rather late in the evening when the last teacher finally heaved a sigh and shut her door. All that could be ready in the time we had was done. Still no playground equipment, but that wouldn't be a problem, I assured myself.

I didn't sleep well that night. I lay in bed and considered what we were embarking upon. I recalled one significant, recent conversation we had as a staff and board. We had been discussing a variety of business items, including the school's name. Debbie Quist, Shirley's daughter and the main teacher for our three older students, had been doing some thinking along those lines already.

"Let's call it 'Logos.' That's Greek for 'word,' and I think that would be far more appropriate than 'Moscow Christian School.'"

We had already decided on the motto of "A Classical and Christian School," based on our agreement with Dorothy Sayer's points on the Trivium in her article, *The Lost Tools of Learning.*

"Logos has the double entendre of a reference to classical roots, as well as Jesus being referred to as the Word of God in John," Debbie went on.

Doug added, "If we're going to use 'Logos,' let's just call it 'Logos School,' versus 'Logos Christian School.'" That doesn't sound very good, and seems rather redundant to boot."

Thus the school was christened. No fanfare, no great announcement. Just a name that sounded appropriate to the small group who would see the school out of the starting blocks. Logos School. Short, easy ... I liked it, too.

Tuesday morning. The first day. I unlocked the glass front doors of the church (the school wouldn't have its own entrance until next year). The teachers arrived early and so we gathered for a brief time in the kindergarten room for prayer and final notes. Where to eat lunch? Who's got the first recess? Shall we all get together for an assembly first? What's an "assembly?" After a brief explanation by the teachers...." Um, yes, let's meet in the fellowship hall at about 9:00 for a short assembly."

I'm not sure what we each expected the first day to be like. I thought it would be something like slowly, but gradually idling back a revved up engine, until you heard just the quiet, smooth hum of a happy motor. It was almost anti-climatic in a way. The day began and then, well, just went on. Quietly, with no need to idle the noise back or anything. I wandered professionally about the only hall, ever-ready to leap into action should a teacher holler for help with a nasty pencil sharpener. But no such cries issued forth, so I returned to my office to see what my secretary was doing.

The first recess came and all seventeen kids trickled out to the grassy area behind the church. The entire staff came out, too, to enjoy the sight of happy children playing and laughing in the warm September sun. The staff had to wait for a while for such a sight. The kids were happy, I guess. However, for the first few minutes, the inaugural recess took on all the jovial appearance of a doctor's waiting room. Every child's face silently was asking the same question: What do we do now? What, in point of fact, was there to do? Restlessness and confusion hung heavily in the air. The kids looked a bit lost, too.

Finally, someone, somewhere obtained a real ball, and no lost desert traveler leaped on a flask of water with more enthusiasm than those kids did leaping on that single ball. Its presence energized all the kids, even those unable to get their hands on it. The boys especially, once the novelty of the first ball wore off, found that the weedy hillside was an undiscovered Aladdin's cave of treasures. In weeks to come they found it be rich and full of wildlife. They could echo Lewis and Clark's sentiments, "we have come into a great and good country!" (It was too bad the girls would come to feel quite differently about the same area—even when the boys enthusiastically shared their significant findings with the ladies, such as healthy garter snakes.)

The first lunch was eaten in the respective classrooms. Later we would set up a couple of tables in the fellowship hall and eat all together.

After lunch, I had the opportunity to introduce our three older students, one each in fifth, sixth and ninth grades, to the history and art I would be teaching them. It felt more like a committee than a class, but we got off to a good start anyway. Among the four of us teachers we covered all the older students' various subjects. The fact that Jim, our ninth grader, would be taught by his older sister was a concern before school began, but once the work actually started there was never any awkwardness.

Three o'clock came and so did the parents to retrieve their offspring. Each parent came equipped with the same two questions: To their child—"Did you have a good time?", and to the teacher and/or me, "How did it go?" To the first question, the answers were varied, but the ones I overheard were relatively positive: "OK, but mom, there isn't much to play with." To the second question, the answers were very similar: "It went really well!", accompanied by sighs of relief. We had begun. The first day was finished, learning had actually occurred, the parents hadn't been disappointed, and only one student had thrown up. Not bad.

CHAPTER THREE

Board Diplomacy: "Wise As Serpents..."

First, I think it advisable for me to justify my audacity to speak authoritatively on this topic, not being currently a board member myself. My experience comes not just from two decades of closely working with (and in our early years, on) the Logos School board. Through no fault of my own, I have also had the pleasure and pain of observing and frequently corresponding with literally dozens of school boards around the nation, particularly boards of classical, Christian schools. I have also read a number of articles by guys who have also worked with school boards. And, lo and behold, the essential elements, good and bad, are eerily similar. So, you may disregard the following points, but mark this—you do so at your own peril! A smart administrator needs to know the heights and pitfalls his board must negotiate. Note: This is not a section for administrators to use as an I-told-you-so weapon and thrust it under the noses of his board. If you do, you are disqualified from expecting respect from those under YOU.

Three points of foundational understandings about boards

First point: A board will either lead its school to growth or to destruction, moving ahead or sliding back, there are no other options. Apart from the grace of God itself operating in your school, no other greater power exists for good or ill in your institution. Perhaps an ill-placed NATO strike could cause more obvious damage, but never underestimate the power of the board.

Second point: There are some unavoidable, critical elements necessary for an effective board. Just as we like to point new Christian school teachers to the excellent resources in *The 7 Laws of Teaching* (original version), due to the timeless, universal truths contained therein, there are common truths that affect every board. And, since we want to be effective, it seems prudent to attend to some of the truths that will push us in that direction.

Third point: It takes time and consistency to become an effective board. Due to the sense of urgency we all share for properly educating our kids, there is a tremendous pressure on classical school boards to get it all right, right away! Board members are people, too, and can therefore easily succumb to the tyranny of the urgent, but this is the birthplace of many personal and structural problems. Our Lord's use of the term "enduring" is very apropos here. Nothing really good will come really fast, except maybe Italian sports cars. Hunker down for the long haul, 'cause that's what it takes!

Fun with our Adamic nature: Some common ailments afflicting boards

As in a marriage or raising children, many seemingly (or actually) complicated problems boards face have common and rather plain sources. An all-too frequent one is a lack of commitment to require board members to act scripturally, most often allowing gossip to go unchecked. Remember what James and Peter say about the tongue. There must be something to it. Other fire-starters include (obviously these are true for you and the staff, too):

1. Assuming motives—"Yes, I know what you said, but I don't think it was what you really meant!"
2. Hearing and acting on only one side of the story—Proverbs says the first man's story sounds very good until you hear the second guy's. Gee, now you have to be Solomon.

3. The Matthew 18 process (going first to the primary person involved to check the story) is ignored—"Say," says a sincere board member as the meeting is winding up, "I got a call from Mrs. Freep and she says that her Bertram told her that the second grade is going on a field trip to a nudist colony. She's not keen on the idea, to put it mildly. Should we discuss that now?" The administrator should have a chance to do some research first.

4. No vested interest in the school (e.g. having children in another school, or not having any children in the school). This is not as direct a line to sin as the other examples above, but it can cause divisiveness and loyalties can be called into question. More importantly, what philosophical or biblical support is there for a board member to have his children in a government school? I have heard some of the standard excuses ... they are lame at best. While it's not a fellowship-denying issue, it certainly should be carefully scrutinized because it does involve a leadership issue.

5. Prayerlessness—i.e. not praying enough as a board, not praying specifically, and/or not praying biblically. There is a scriptural model and the board should follow it.

6. Private agendas/party spirit—These can be acted out or just carried around and trotted out frequently—"Well, I've talked with a number of parents about this and others have sought me out. They want me to represent their feelings to the board and I promised them that's just what I would do!" If a good number of parents seem to know exactly which board member will be sympathetic to their specific concerns, the party spirit is alive and well in your school. I call these board members "lightening rods" as they seem to attract the high voltage gossip. Yup, there's that problem again. Remember, the board is not the House of Representatives!

7. Improper meetings of the board, e.g. a few, select board members with each other or with select parents—did I men-

tion gossip already? Good. "Sharing concerns" is frequently a softer synonym for "gossip." But a stink weed by any other name doesn't smell like a rose. Well, you have the idea.

8. The treatment of administrator not being up to snuff. More specifically:
   - The board using the old '80s micro-management techniques. Another way of describing this approach is breathing over the administrator's shoulder. The board must create good, clear policies and then leave to it to the administrator to enact them. Accountability doesn't mean microscopic scrutiny of his every move or decision.
   - Not providing professional support—Are notable accomplishments by the administrator (and other staff members) publicly and privately recognized by the board?
   - Does the board provide the administrator encouragement to grow in understanding and application of a classical vision? This isn't just looking for the evasive "Atta-boys," but rather providing the critical direction and reinforcement the administrator needs for doing his job.
9. Does the board understand the unique bridge that the administrator is between the board's vision/goals and the implementation at the staff/school level of those goals? Their demonstrable trust in him (you) should make their understanding on this clear.
10. Budget health—Financial worries can be the root of all sorts of evil. The administrator plays a key role in brainstorming ideas for meeting money problems. But the board must assume full responsibility for those problems. (Sadly, they rarely get the credit for solving the problems, unless YOU point that out to folks.)
11. Parent contentment/communication both ways—Is the board viewed as a Star Chamber, i.e. an all-knowing, faceless group of people meeting secretively to mete out judgments?

That perception is almost always present in some form. Here again, in addition to the board's seeking communication with the parents, the administrator can be a big help to the board by providing vehicles for that communication, e.g. newsletter space.

12. Lack of adherence to and advocacy of the primary elements of the school's founding vision/philosophy,
13. I.e. driving off the road—While new board members should be voted in and their good ideas welcomed, they should be committed to the original vision of the school. Certain founding ideas are not up for grabs. Unlike the U.S. Supreme Court during the last half-century, the school board should be strict constructionists of their "constitution."
14. Structural problems—Ignoring Robert's Rules of Order (the "oil" for smooth working), having too many members, having too few, male vs. female roles not understood biblically and practically (more on this later), board member qualifications not clear, meeting too often, not meeting often enough, meetings run too long ... yadda, yadda, yadda (that's Hebrew for etc.) It is very possible to wear good people out and scare off good replacements by doing dumb things year in and year out.
15. Lack of emphasis on biblical unity—Even if you have a school that is run by one church (not always the best option), there will be times that try men's souls and unity will be strained, and even broken at times. Open discussion and commitment to unity above all other school issues is a must. Our Lord said the pagans will know He came by how His children demonstrate love for each other. This love will be severely tried in the crucible of board meetings.

Whew! And those are just the most obvious problems that can arise. Perhaps you have some nuances to add. Again, the above list should not be used by you as a stick to whack (even mentally) your board with, as it suits you. If anything, now that you are in the know, you could/

should use the above information to help educate your board members. Constantly remind yourself of three things as you work with your board:

- Almost without exception, the members want the school to succeed, just like you do.
- They are not as much in the know about the school as you are, even if they think they are.
- You are their servant (i.e. humble resource person) and need to act like it!

So, help them by respectfully educating them while you serve them. The results can be quite satisfying:

What is common among effective boards?

Lest you may have been discouraged by the above list, remember, it is possible to do it right. Not surprisingly, the right things are pretty much the positive image of the negatives presented above. The following characteristics indicate a maturing, godly board.

1. The board keeps its own "house" in order—It recognizes the Scripture's authority/admonitions/principles regarding requirements for board members, i.e. qualifications for leadership in our schools are similar to the qualifications for elder and deacon. Although board members do not serve exactly the same functions, the kinds of issues they have to deal with in the school are not too dissimilar to those facing elders and deacons at times. On a very basic level, there should certainly be no compromise in terms of marriage and family obligations (including the behavior of children!), as necessary for leadership.
2. Adheres to godly standards of behavior, in and out of meetings. For example, the principles found in Matthew 18 apply to school boards and individual members. Fellowship standards are also non-negotiable. Did I mention gossip already? Good.
3. Understands the requirements for and commitment to

Christian education. All board members who have school-age children, if at all possible, should have them enrolled. There are sometimes extenuating circumstances, e.g. the school doesn't offer the necessary grades or the child has handicaps the school can't address. But simply stated, board members need to be willing to put their children where their mouths and opinions are—it only makes sense. It also demonstrates a public commitment to the school. Having adults without enrolled children on the board may have certain technical advantages (e.g. someone with business savvy), but you are looking toward the long-term fulfillment of your vision, remember?

4. Recognizes Christ's Lordship in discussions, planning, and regular prayer. Yes, prayer should always be part of the agenda. But fruitful prayers are only possible in reality if #1. is seriously adhered to, i.e. the board is truly filled with men* of God and His word.

5. The board insists on professional standards of behavior in meetings, i.e. Roberts' Rules (modified as befits a less formal situation). Every machine with moving, working parts needs some lubricant to smooth rough surfaces and to cool heated, friction-inducing actions. "Mr. Chairman, I would like to move...," seconded, discussed, and passed, and then on to the next item. This seemingly stilted process can keep issues from becoming personal battles, not to mention the requisite good record-keeping.

6. The board treats you, the administrator, respectfully and professionally. Obviously that means you have to attend the board meetings to receive that kind of treatment. Why wouldn't you? They're your boss. Note: You have one boss, not one in every board member. The board defers to its "primary resource" (that's you). Remember, no one else should

* Yup, there it is again. See the comments about women administrators under Qualifications. Those apply to board members, too.

know the school better. You are to respect their authority and governance; they respect your knowledge by asking and listening, a lot! Even if they then vote against your advice. You've done your job.

7. Works from published,timely agenda. The board chairman usually publishes the agenda a week ahead of time. This helps avoid the syndrome of "Hey guys, guess what I heard...!" headlining the board's meeting, and away they go. Fascinating as the latest news item or concern might be, the board needs to stick to listed topics. This not only has the practical benefit of getting the work to be done addressed, it keeps folks from being right about the Star Chamber appearance. Agendas are a public document, and if the public comes to watch the board in action, the public expects to see the document used.

8. Conducts business on the premise of being a "meeting held in public, not a public meeting." Parents with concerns (few otherwise come) may want to express opinions or question the board. But this should be allowed only if they have been planned in the agenda, then follow protocol, i.e. the board listens politely, asks some clarifying questions, then thanks the parent and determines among the board members what to do with the information presented. The public town hall meeting may seem picturesque in a Norman Rockwell painting, but too frequently open, public discussions of problems frequently have all the finesse of a Jerry Springer show. Even in Christian schools. Recite this often in front of the mirror and your board—"We are not a democracy."

9. The board does not shirk from taking the captain's role of a ship, i.e. full responsibility, willing to go down with it, if necessary. Pointing fingers of blame didn't work for Adam or anyone after him, but still we try, not living in age where courage and nobility are frequently modeled. Certainly not everything that goes wrong in the school is the board's specif-

ic fault; it is the board's responsibility, though.

10. Firmly believes that there are no unicorns, goblins, or "board member hats" in this world. In other words, board members cannot carry the authority of board membership with them beyond an official meeting of the board and its recorded directives. Committee work has specific tasks: they are not free-lancing. There should not be any Lone Rangers either, riding out alone seeking truth and justice with all the best of intentions. If you see any of these guys, do your best to kindly shoot them out of the saddle. The board's job IS a team-effort, with very specific, limited authority.

11. Each member sees the necessity of and supports the corporate nature of the board. This follows hard on the heels of the above "no-hat" idea, but more specifically regarding all communications from the board, written and verbal, to you, and to parents, or to the broader community. When the board determines, by official action, to approve a communique, it then becomes the entire board's view and message. Individual members may not publicly distance themselves from unpleasant decisions by implying or saying, "Well, don't blame me, I voted against that!" That's not just poor leadership, it is an unbiblical view of submission.

12. The wise board knows and uses proper avenues for addressing constituents' concerns and questions. The board publicizes (through handbooks, newsletters) the proper means to address the board: when, where, and how. All issues need to have your input, heads-up for information and the building of trust. The board shouldn't normally hear about or know something that you don't.

13. Each member should be willing to make hard decisions regarding financial, personnel issues affecting the school's health. No waffling is allowed; the buck stops there. It can get very hard—you are dealing with people's lives in many instances—all the more reason to do the above,especially sat-

urating all with prayer and deferring to biblical (not always pragmatic) principles.

14. The mature board seeks to make as informed decisions as possible. Proverbs espouses consulting wise help, not just relying only on past experiences, ("We've never done it that way before!") nor responding in a knee-jerk reaction. The James' admonition about slow to speak and quick to listen is a good by-word for the board (and you). The board's adopting this practice, though, may cause it to appear to move at the pace of a tortoise when you want action, now! So, if it's a choice between prompt decisions being made in ignorance, or slow deliberations that cause you to squirm with impatience, I recommend learning to squirm quietly and respectfully.

15. The wise board understands the critical necessity of being an advocate, corporately and individually, for the school's classical vision. Some practical ways this shows up:

    - Each member should be able to articulate the primary distinctives of the school's classical goals. This takes individual (not just collective) initiative and willingness to become educated on goals/vision. Books should be read, visits should be made to the school (an annual Board Visitation Day works well for us), and possibly visits to other classical schools. (Remember, all this takes time.)
    - Policies are subjected to scrutiny in light of the school's classical goals (as appropriate) during an annual, pain-staking review. There should always be a willingness to learn and adapt, and admit change is necessary. This, by the way, gets harder, not easier, the longer you operate. Change for change's sake is not the point—a joyful embracing of better ways of doing what your vision directs is the point.
    - Staff hirings and evaluations of the school reflect the board's commitment to classical education. Our structure has the board hire those in authority over kids (teachers/

admin) and then only by unanimous vote. Again, there is wisdom in collective counsel. The hiring and evaluation documents and procedures the board approves should obviously reinforce specific goals and philosophies of school.

BOARD COMPOSITION

Permanent members (formerly Founding Members): In our board structure and history, we began with four "founding" board members. Several years after the school began, we added two more founding members. As time went on, finding people who had been with the school since it began became problematic. So, the members who were on the board "for life," i.e. to keep a consistent view of the vision, were referred to as "permanent" members. We have five of them now, with one going off for a sabbatical each year. When one of these members steps down, only the board members (all of them) get to vote on a replacement.

Elected members: We changed our by-laws in 1990 to include the election process and placement of three elected board members who would be on staggered three year terms. The nominees must be supported by at least two seated board members and pass the board interview to be put on the ballot. The ballots go to our school association, which we define as being made up of current families, half to full time staff, and board members.

So, at any given time, we have seven seated board members: four permanent and three elected. (Typically the board chairman moderates but doesn't vote, except to break a tie.) Every July, one permanent member goes on sabbatical, another comes back on, and an elected member is replaced by the winner of the election. A frequent question we get is if there is often a split between the views of the permanent members and the elected? I cannot recall ever seeing that happen. Opinions are held by individuals and don't seem to be affected by their term length on the board.

Meetings Of Note

Some vague sense, nibbling at the edge of my awareness, told me this was going to be a slightly different board meeting than the usual fare. Perhaps it was the way Larry Lucas, our board chairman, firmly called the meeting to order; or maybe it was the extremely crowded conditions; or just maybe it was the fact that we were gathered for our meeting in a two-seated, open carriage being pulled by a very large black horse. Otherwise it was pretty much business as usual.

We had initially gathered, as we did for many weeks, in Larry's downtown, downstairs office. At that time I was not only the principal, but also one of six board members. John Sawyer and Bill Twigg, both dads in Logos, had been asked to serve as permanent board members in 1984. They accepted this burden cheerfully, and came on to help guide the growing school. We were still meeting weekly (!) at that time, and, as mentioned, often in Larry's accounting office. He served well and long as our chairman for quite a few years.

This week, among other items, the board would be discussing the acceptance of a deaf boy, what to do about low income and high bills (a standard agenda item for numerous years), and the hiring of several needed staff members. Bill, a wheelwright by trade, had arrived in his carriage on this beautiful late-summer afternoon.

"Say," Larry blurted, just as we were sitting down to grind through the work ahead, "Why don't we have the meeting in Bill's buggy and get a ride at the same time?"

That was Larry; all business, from top to bottom. And since Bill would be the last person to insist on decorum, it was pretty quickly a done deal. To be fair, I don't believe any of us strongly objected to a buggy ride, vs. staying and working in a stuffy office.

Bill took the reins in his leathery hands, gave a small chirrup, and we were off at a nice walking pace through and out of downtown Moscow. In spite of being stared at and feeling like something in a Macy's Day parade, we actually got some work completed. We headed out of town toward Bill's shop, and would car pool back to the office from there.

As we clopped along the main road heading out of town near Les Schwab Tires, we were in the thick of discussing acceptance of the deaf boy. Suddenly the carriage jolted as Charlie (the horse) shied at some unseen object in the ditch. Fearing for his life, I suppose, he then broke into a rather awkward canter. At the same time, one of the braces attaching the carriage to Charlie fell off, rendering the reins virtually useless to Bill. America's Funniest Home Videos hadn't been thought up yet, so we were the only ones to enjoy every moment of a real-life, run-away horse and carriage, in the mid-1980's, for goodness sake. "Enjoy" may be the wrong word there, since, speaking for myself, scared spit-less more or less described my feelings.

My life didn't pass before my eyes, but every western movie scene of runaway carriages did:

LONG DISTANCE SHOT: Foam-flecked horses drag rickety carriage, filled with screaming minor role, pioneer—actors, along dangerous, rock-filled road.

CUT TO CLOSE SHOT: Terror-filled faces of expendable pioneers.

CUT TO CLOSE SHOT: Riders behind carriage racing to stop horses.

CUT TO CLOSE-UP: Back wheel of carriage starts fiercely wobbling.

CUT TO GROUND SHOT, ANGLE UP: Carriage approaches nasty bend in road at about 150 mph.

CUT TO MEDIUM DISTANCE SHOT, GROUND LEVEL: Horses reach bend, execute neat slice to right; carriage reaches bend, fails to execute neat slice; separates from horses (NO ANIMALS WERE HARMED TO MAKE THIS MOVIE); carriage hits rock, back wheel flies off; carriage and settlers flip skyward over conveniently placed high cliff ... scream volume UP.

Nevertheless, Bill stayed calm, and called firmly to Charlie to take it easy. Charlie dragged us across an unoccupied (providentially) intersection and up into the Les Schwab lot, where the slight incline, along with our considerable weight, slowed him to a halt. For once, the "Fast Action Team" at Les Schwab didn't dash out to help us; actually they seemed a bit nonplused at finding a carriage-full of very pale people at their doorstep, so to speak.

Bill fixed up the carriage in no time, Charlie got his attitude straight, and we had a rather pleasant, uneventful ride out to the country. We even finished our business in record time. And we all really enjoyed Larry's stuffy office the next week.

The board meetings weren't always as fun as the carriage ride. For one thing, it took us literally years to figure out that, by meeting every week, the board was "micro-managing". That was an eighties term for sweating the small stuff. But we were all learning, albeit slowly, what everyone's job was supposed to be. The board was essentially acting as another administrator, since I would bring to them just about every minor or major piece of business affecting the school. Being kind souls, they would seek to guide me, when what we all needed was someone to say, "Just make a policy and tell the principal to figure out how to apply it!"

Friends In Time of Need

Thankfully, we did have some specific people turn up from time to time who helped us along the path of maturing as a school. One such person, to whom we are greatly indebted, was Mr. Allen Cumings. I had had the privilege of first hearing and meeting Allen at one of the annual A.C.S.I. (Association of Christian Schools, Intl.) conventions in Seattle. He was doing a series of seminars on development and school financing. He made the mistake of offering to help any school that would be interested in having him come. "Mistake" because I quickly obtained his number and address, and then, after receiving my board's permission, invited him to come to Logos to share his insights with us.

Allen was working in Portland, Oregon, with a ministry to police officers. He was also very much in demand as a development adviser for businesses and educational institutions. We were very fortunate to be able to get him so quickly and easily. Our board members took time off their work schedules and spent a whole day with Allen. He had already looked over our newsletters, budget, and other financial documents, and told us what he thought of them. He was polite, but candid. For instance, at one point, he held up a copy of our newsletter and said, "Now, would you really want to read this?"

Since I was the primary author of that epistle, I had to resist the temptation to say, "Well, yeah!" He had made a good point though. It was boring. Actually he made quite a few good points, not only about how to improve our newsletters, but also about our payroll: "You need to pay your teachers much more than you are and there is no excuse for not seeking to do so!"

The day was extremely profitable for the board primarily and for the school in general, as the board began to implement Allen's wise counsel. In later years, we turned to him a number of times for practical assistance. Development became a critical element to establishing Logos School's support network, and we gained much insight into development work because of Allen's generous and practical guidance. (This was a wonderful example to us when, many years later, other schools and individuals looked to us for some guidance.)

Another gentleman who spoke "a fitting word" to us, though in a much briefer time, was Dr. Bob Smith. He arrived one morning, unannounced and unexpected, as a guest of Jim Wilson, who also was popping in to our morning staff meeting. Dr. Smith was at that time an elderly, well-known evangelist. Jim Wilson is also an evangelist, a pastor, Doug's father, and a long-time friend of my family. Dr. Smith and Jim didn't stay long that day, but Dr. Smith was there long enough to touch upon a very critical issue I had been wrestling with, unbeknownst to him. He had had a good exposure to many Christian schools, he said, and he wanted us to be clear on one thing in our work:

"You will have to decide," he said quietly, but firmly, "whether you will be a school that primarily assists Christian parents in training up their children in the Lord, or if you will be a school that primarily reaches out to unsaved, and troubled kids. You have to decide which because you cannot successfully do both." (See *Chapter 5—Families/Gate Keeping.*)

His comment struck home. I was amazed, and profoundly thankful, both then and to this day. Whether he knew it or not, Dr. Smith had summed up a major conflict we were experiencing in those early years. In our naivete, we had assumed that since we were about God's "business," using the Bible and prayer and everything, we could not only educate, but spiritually straighten out just about any kid that came along. To our dismay, we learned the hard way that not only could we not "spiritually straighten" them out, too often these troubled kids began to negatively affect the "good" kids.

Though the ramifications were not comfortable to contemplate, the decision was not difficult to make. We had started with the purpose of being a Christian school. The board had set our six primary, mission-defining goals in 1984. Though we still would accept non-Christian families into Logos, our focus would be to train all our students from a Biblical perspective. If a family or student was unwilling or unable to accept this purpose, Logos would not be the school for them. This decision, based on our goals, clarified our acceptance policies, and that in turn, certainly set the tone for our student body for many years to come. There were times when my heart literally ached for parents who had come to our school since they "had no other place to go" for help with their rebellious student. But unless there was an obvious desire and commitment to change, that student would have to be turned away. We could not, and would not, do what the parents had been unable, or unwilling to do, for their own child.

Keeping Classical

As we continued to seek to build Logos from a vision into reality, it was inevitable that clashes of the "best" means to accomplish this would occur. These clashes often occurred at our board meetings, as with the best interest of the kids in each of our hearts, we sought to implement our various ideas. Many times it was the philosophical equivalent of trying to park six cars in a two-car garage; they just weren't all going to fit. Nevertheless, it was important to trot out our individual thoughts, toss them around, and pray that iron would sharpen iron. By God's grace it actually did more often than it didn't.

A very significant theme, the classical aspect of Logos, was not only the toughest and vaguest one to get a grip on, it was also the most controversial among our school parents. The time came when, in response to a number of parental concerns expressed to the board regarding "this classical thing," we decided to hold an informational meeting. This was aimed primarily at our slowly growing number of secondary parents. Their kids were getting rather hefty reading assignments in "primary sources" which the kids couldn't begin to comprehend, along with large amounts of homework. All done in the name of a classical education, as it was being defined by the individual ideas of the secondary teachers. To be fair, the secondary teachers had received only hazy, broad directions from the school as to how to implement the classical method.

So, not too surprisingly, the parents came to the meeting ready to slice and dice the classical idea; the board and I came with vague reassurances and grand visions. A collision of fairly immense proportions should have been predictable. We weren't good at predicting, and while not quite the Battle of Little Big Horn, it was still rather messy. Everything from scrapping the secondary program entirely to scrapping the entire idea of a classical education was put forth, with feeling. The message was very clearly sent—stick to just being a "normal Christian school" (whatever that meant)!

The next morning I was still stinging from some of the remarks and tone of the meeting. For not the first or last time, I felt our "grand experiment" as I often called Logos in private with Julie, was on the rocks. Where would Logos School go, how would it move ahead, if we didn't have the support of our families? Should we really toss out the idea of a classical education? Maybe it really was a pipe-dream. After all, even Dorothy Sayers never actually made a school based on her ideas, did she? Maybe she knew that in reality, with twentieth-century kids and culture, it would never fly. It was just too weird, archaic, and unrealistic.

Such were my despondent thoughts and feelings. Nevertheless, once again the Lord gave the board members more peace and wisdom than I had. After quite a few serious and quite vigorous meetings, the board determined to not only keep the idea of a full K-12 program, it reaffirmed its commitment to a classical education. Though we couldn't know it then, this was a watershed for the school. We never again pondered turning back from our original vision.

CHAPTER FOUR

Staff Considerations

So, you've got a pretty good idea of the kind of school you want and you've evaluated the skills, or at least the enthusiasm, you personally bring to the table, so to speak. You know who you work for (answer: the board) and you should have a fair idea of the board's tasks and make-up so that you can best serve them and the school. (This is a brief review, lest you may have missed the point. Review being the seventh law of teaching, but we'll get to that later.) In short, you have a pretty good idea of what you want to do. Now, borrowing a metaphor from The Little Red Hen, who will help you make the bread? You'll need lots of qualified help and, not to put too fine a point on it, the smartest thing we administrators can do is to find staff members who are far more able to teach than we are.

Hence, our first task in this regard is to find them and then get them hired....

HIRING STAFF

"Staff" within the following context refers only to teaching and administration personnel. Support staff members, e.g. secretaries, librarians, custodians, etc. are also critical elements of and contributors to the school's mission. Everyone working in the school is a teacher to the kids, therefore everyone must be redeemed, as well as understand the vision of the school. But let's not pretend we're egalitarians—the primary purpose we administrators, as well as all the other support staff members serve, is to help the teachers do their job. They are the front line warriors; we are the supply and medical corps. They need us to assist them because they are the ones who face the daily battles.

"Where do you find all those wonderful people?"

When folks visit Logos for the first time and observe some of my teachers, they frequently ask the question above. If they are from another classical Christian school, they often ask that question with the same expression as that of a hungry diner who asks the waiter what he might recommend from the menu. I know what they're thinking: they want my teachers for their school! Things can turn ugly at that point. But most people, particularly our parents, just greatly appreciate our instructors. Simply put, we have been blessed by truly remarkable teachers who have contributed many years of personal investment to make Logos the school it is. How can you get teachers like them, without trying to steal mine?

Well, you have to know what you're looking for: Job descriptions, along with desirable personal aspects, need to be thoroughly considered and written down. Paperwork, my friend, paperwork. Not much fun, I know, but very necessary at this juncture. When applicants pick up an application, it should be the first step to training them, so it should be packed with questions and information for both parties. In other words, be aware of what they're looking for:

Women—Generally, they want a job with clear purposes and adequate internal support (that means they want to count on you to back them up, in every situation). They like lots of specifics in the necessary materials, instructions, and expectations. And they thrive in a pleasant working environment. If they are married, their husbands are to be deferred to, as appropriate. If they are single, their dads' opinions should be respected.

Men—Generally, they want a job with a clear vision and a challenge, and at least adequate support for a family. If they have a growing family, this may be a bit tough but with some creative ideas for additional work, it can be done. Mainly, they want to trust you to understand and work with them to meet their family's needs. But they also really like the ability to help shape and build a program.

(WARNING: In our experience to date, we have not been able to retain a single (vs. married) young man for more than two years. We either have had to fire them, or they have moved on, being footloose and fancy-free. In a few rare instances, they have gotten married within that time frame, which has served to steady them a bit, and make them more fit for use. You have been warned.)

FINDING THESE PEOPLE

It will be necessary to establish and define the "circles" wherein you might find potential applicants for staff positions. Those below are suggested in priority and population size (smallest to largest) order:

- First Circle: Parent constituency—Hands down, parents make the best teachers! They have a vested interest (their kids) in the school's success, they have a better, albeit basic, understanding of the classical, Christian philosophy, they are more likely to give some longevity (a wonderful aspect!) to the program, and they will appreciate the tuition assistance (which should be given to staff members).
- Second Circle: Local churches—Caution here: Choose wisely. At the risk of sounding rude, not every "Christian teacher" should or can be a teacher in a classical, Christian setting. If you've done your homework on the philosophy of classical education, you should know what I am referring to. Christian or not, most teacher-wanna-be's are trained in secular, pathetic colleges of education. Then there is the doctrinal strength, or lack thereof, in their churches to consider. The applicants will bring baggage; you need to know the churches well enough to know what kind of baggage it will be and

whether you can work with it, i.e. is it compatible with the school's philosophy?

- Third Circle: Regional Christian networks/National Christian networks—Some examples here would obviously include the Association of Classical Christian Schools (ACCS), as well as the Association of Christian Schools, International (ACSI), Inter-Christo, etc. Here again, however, let the buyer beware. The comments about churches in your area are tripled when it comes to this level of contact. To keep it simple, the further you have to reach geographically for a teacher, the more inherent dangers there are. It is just plain hard to get to know someone long-distance and short-term. Remember, you are trusting this person with the most precious people on this planet, according to their parents. So thoroughly check out any organizations, read their publications, get all the paper work you can on each applicant, and even if they look really great on paper, don't settle for anything less than a face-to-face interview (it may cost money, but too bad).

Of course there are pluses and minuses with each Circle. A couple examples here may suffice to convince you that nothing comes easy. Parent-teachers are usually great, but they can be too close to the situation to be objective when they need to be. Also, removing a poor teacher who also happens to be a parent is a double whammy. You will probably also lose their kids and likely incur some harmful gossip. Sorry to sound so negative: I'm just going by a fair number of observations.

On the other hand, a plus we have seen with a long-distance hire was that he came with an incredible zeal for and knowledge of classical education. He wanted us and we quickly determined we wanted him, even though he was from California.

Still, generally speaking, "home-grown" are indeed best. In certain instances, you may find you have a need for a specially trained teacher, such as for Latin, and there are none on any horizon. We have found it advantageous to look down the road, so to speak, and anticipate the need, then seek someone nearby we can train to fill that need in due time. This may not be as hard as it sounds; establish good communications with your parents and supportive churches and you will be amazed at the contacts you make!

Initial Screening, or the first hurdles

Application procedures, documents—Back to the paperwork and process for a moment: Everyone needs to clearly understand who does what, when, and with what paperwork. For instance, we require a lot of writing by the applicant, including specific background info, a testimony, transcripts, supervisor references, etc. This not only tells us a good deal about the person, it lets us see how well they write! Then we call the references personally. This is very helpful since former employers will often be more willing to speak more candidly than what is written in a reference, not to mention verifying the validity of the references; one time we discovered a reference had been dead for two years! Whoops.

Initial interview—Contrary to common wisdom, first impressions and appearances do matter, so follow your gut. How's that for sage advice? Yes, it's good and necessary to have a thorough list of questions and make notes of answers, but honestly, when all has been said and written, your basic impression of the person should carry a great amount of weight. If you have initial misgivings, listen to them and examine them carefully. As time has gone by, I have developed the ability to generally know, usually within ten minutes, whether or not this person in front of me is someone whom I would wish to have on my staff. The cover of the book may not say it all, but it says something.

Second meeting—Once you determine this is indeed someone you think you'd like to pursue, then communicate all the basic aspects of the school and job—vision, authority, requirements, finances—in this second interview. Even so, you can be sure you will leave something out. That's okay. You will get better at it as you go along. The point is, you don't want to spend a lot of time with someone you won't be recommending to the board. If you do want to recommend this person, then give him the best picture of the work that you can. Oh yes, you might want to ensure the applicant knows your school's hiring process, i.e. what comes next.

Board (or Personnel Committee) Interview

In our situation, the entire board makes the final decision for hiring after they interview the applicant. Prior to that interview, a few thoughts to consider:

- Only the best applicants go to this level. Why bring second-round draft choices to the board for presentation? The board wants to know you will be thrilled to have this person work for you. If you're hesitant, who will reassure them?
- Be sure to get the applicant's materials to members ahead of time. This gives the board members a chance to review them prior to meeting the person face-to-face. An obvious idea, you say? True, but from what I've heard, you will be in the minority, but that's good.
- The board should have a rather comprehensive list of questions (see appendix). Don't let them use leading questions, e.g. "Do you prefer a well-ordered classroom?" Duh. Or "Do you like children?" "No, not really, but the salary package is very attractive to me." Believe it or not, with a few new board members over the years, I have heard similar obvious questions. Ask questions that require the applicant to provide examples or explanations. Planning, planning.
- Allow for applicants' questions—the kind and number will tell you and the board more about the way this person thinks. They really should have some. Remember the point about your forgetting certain items during the first interview? I have found applicants often have a keen ability to ask the board things I forgot to address. Humbling, but very necessary.
- When all has been said and it's time for the board vote, I recommend the requirement we have held to since we began. That is, a unanimous vote being best. It requires and reinforces the kind of unanimity the board should seek always. An important cautionary note is appropriate here: Don't let expediency drive decisions. That's true at just about any time;

clear principles should always drive and urgency should take a back seat. But it's especially critical at hiring times. Late August, for instance, is a terrible time to have to make hiring decisions. The pressure to cave on dubious concerns will be immense. Take your time and encourage the board to do the same—just about every time we have "blinked," as I call it, and hired a less than sure-fire applicant, we have usually come to regret it.

EVALUATING STAFF

What are evaluations meant to do, and what aren't they meant to do? Good question. Fundamentally, you evaluate your staff because they need you to. The Bible regards as foolish those who would measure themselves by themselves, and yet you might be amazed by the number of Christian schools where accountability of any sort is almost nil. Maybe you wouldn't be amazed, but I have been. The leadership just assumes that no objective "outside" measure is necessary, I guess. Sometimes it's just a matter of being unwilling to take the time and effort.

However, most often, teachers want to know how they're doing and they want to do a better job. That's why you take the time and trouble to evaluate them. A good evaluation provides feedback on tasks well done and ways to improve. Rather than a lack of trust, as some may allege evaluations imply, it displays your trust in the teachers' desire to improve. And, when done well, it displays the teacher's trust in you. You are on their side so they do not feel threatened, but rather welcome you into their rooms.

Evaluations are not primarily done to weed out the poor teachers. True, when necessary, documentation from evaluations is a critical element in determining if a poor teacher should be let go, sometimes even before the year ends. But, prior to that decision, the hope and purpose of the evaluations are that they would assist the poor teacher to become a retained, better teacher.

Put simply, evals are done to:

- Direct staff improvement, ascertain retention and possible advancement, if such a path is desired and available, e.g. to an administrative position. But don't advance someone past the best use of their skills.
- Generate school improvement—furthering the widespread, growing application of your school's philosophy. The teachers put feet on the philosophy through their daily application of it, and the evidence in the children's learning. Proud parents will talk to other parents about their children's teachers.
- Demonstrate accountability to those in authority over us, which is both scriptural and necessary as we acknowledge the parental oversight of our work. It fosters the attitude of a willingness to learn more, even after years of teaching.

Some necessary prerequisites for your evaluation program to work well

School Philosophy, Goals: These obviously need to be written and appropriately promulgated in the staff handbook, as well as more public documents. As with everything else done in the school, the evaluations of teachers should be a logical, direct by-product of the school's philosophy.

Job Description/Evaluation Tool: These are tied together and should reflect the school goals, as well as be put in the staff handbook (there should be no hidden agendas or standards for evaluation). For instance, *The Seven Laws of Teaching*, by John M. Gregory (the original edition), are an unparalleled, excellent measure and can be spelled out in a tool quite easily.

Administrator-staff member relationship: It should go without saying, but it won't, that an already well-established relationship exists, based on trust and good communications regarding expectations for the teacher.

Legal considerations: These are necessary to give some thought to, sad to say, in our litigatious society, but the above documentation, combined with all your actions and words being above board and documented, should be adequate for most situations.

Here is a suggested process

Planning/Pre-Conference—This is particularly helpful with new teachers, to discuss the reasons for and process of the evaluation. It can also be helpful with experienced teachers to identify any areas of particular concern they would like you to observe and help them address (you see how the trust factor is working there?). To set the visits up, I just send around a sign-up sheet for times (their first and second choices) the teachers would like me to come. I send back a confirmation. I realize this means they will know when I am coming and can plan an "exceptional" lesson. So what? Why shouldn't I give them a chance to show what they can do well? Then that becomes the norm I expect and should see (as I tell them) when I pop in informally.

Observation—These take at least a half-hour or slightly more. I like to observe the start, middle, and end of a complete lesson. The teacher usually has a chair in the back for me and I tell them ahead of time that I will be making notes for myself of what they're doing; not how well, just the specific teaching acts.

Analyze/Write-Up—I then use the notes I took to consider how the teacher is doing compared to the specific things we discussed together ahead of time, as well as compared to the job description and philosophy of our school. Specific examples from my observations are helpful to the teacher to get across a commendation or recommendation.

Set objectives for next time—These too go on the form the teacher sees and they should be rather specific, for everyone's sake.

Post-observation Meeting: After I give the teacher the written evaluation, we set a time for a short conference. This face-to-face time is very important to give them encouragement and more direction, as well as to answer any questions they have about the evaluation or other topics.

Costs/Benefits

As with everything you do at school, there are costs related to doing teacher evaluations. There aren't any real monetary costs I've discovered, but there is a definite cost in your time. It is tempting, especially as you get a more experienced staff, to forego or put off doing evaluations since they take a lot of time to do. Don't! They are very necessary to the teachers and the school. The benefits aren't as tangible or as fun as buying cool stuff or building projects, but they are far more beneficial to your primary purposes. When done well, evaluations strengthen the bond you have with your teachers and give you a chance to see and promote excellent teaching. Then, when you have the opportunities, you can boast about your teachers with practical illustrations. Don't worry—they'll get over the embarrassment when you do that in public.

"WHY CAN'T A WOMAN BE MORE LIKE A MAN?"—ACKNOWLEDGING AND LIVING WITH THE DIFFERENT GENDERS ON YOUR STAFF

As we sat down for our usual elementary staff meeting one morning in December, I exchanged the typical pleasantries with some of the teachers:

"Say, Debbie, that's a Christmas-y looking blouse."

"Thanks! You know, I bought this at a yard sale last year for ninety-nine cents, just because it had a little stain around this one button and another loose button. I wasn't sure if I would be able to wear it, even after fixing it, but this morning I thought I would just go ahead. It goes well with this sweater, don't you think? Can you see where the stain was?"

This last question was an open inquiry largely directed at the other female teachers who quickly reassured her that, no, they could not see any remains of the stain. This led to a brief discussion of stains and blouses. The two male teachers and I waited patiently and exchanged slightly haunted looks as this topic wound down.

Just for contrast and the fun of it, I then mentioned to one male staff member: "Say, David, classy tie. Is it new?"

"No, it isn't. And you know it."

"True. Well, today we will likely need to have indoor recess...." And on with the other news of the day. Lest there be misunderstanding or wrong assumptions, let me state that, although the teacher was blond, she was one of the sharpest and sweetest teachers it has been my pleasure to work with. But, the point stands—men and women were created as rather different genders of the same species. It behooves a wise administrator to discover the ways they are different, particularly as they are manifest in our work place.

Before I go any further it may be appropriate to enumerate my credentials to even broach this topic. These may give me credibility as a rare, in-the-know guy, or they may condemn me as a guy who, with all the experiences I've had, should've come up with better conclusions. In any case, here are my bona fides:

*I have had a wonderful mother for many years.

*I was the only son of my parents, who also had three daughters, i.e. my sisters.

*I have a wonderful wife of over twenty-five years.

*I have three lovely daughters and, like my parents, I also have only one son.

*I have worked closely with many little girls, young ladies, and adult women for most of my career.

So, yes, I think I am qualified to address this topic and state emphatically that, with apologies to Judy Collins (Joni Mitchell?) "it's female illusions I recall, I really don't know women at all." Like most marvels of creation, the daughters of Eve seldom fail to amaze me with their complexity. To wit, my admitted disclaimer for all generalizations and slight exaggerations to follow. And I freely and thankfully admit I am, by God's grace, a guy.

That all said, due to my unremitting exposure to the gentler sex, I have some observations to share about the Christian school workplace that you might find enlightening.

Major differences defined (in a scientifically loose manner)

A pseudo-scientific denial of biological egalitarianism:

Contrary to the spirit of the age, that is, rampant egalitarianism, God made men and women differently. True, Eve came from Adam's rib, so there are similar DNA patterns which Adam recognized right off the bat, after recovering from his surgery.

But, to use some common computer vernacular, men's and women's mother boards are definitely hard-wired in two distinctly different compositions. For instance, where men have a direct path from input or source to one terminus where a specific action takes place, women have a multitude of possible paths, leading to a variety of terminals, resulting in an action, that may or may not have a similarity to the man's.

To back up my computer analogy with actual biological research (which took place somewhere), real scientists not long ago (I don't know when) did a brain comparison on men and women. They somehow monitored brain activity when the brain was given a stimulus, such as a question being asked to the person. When the man was asked the question, one part (lobe?) of his brain lit up, as seen on the scientific monitors. When asked the same question, the brain of the woman had various lobes light up. So you see, conclusive proof of fundamentally different wiring! I don't recall the scientists' conclusions of all this, but I will take what serves my point here.

Other unique characteristic considerations, at least for our purposes: (Not essentially or inherently good or bad; like most equipment, it's how its used.)

Ladies

Assumptions, intuition, reading between the lines—A woman has an innate ability to perceive what is frequently obscure to a man. This can be very valuable, particularly in working with young children, particularly girls. The very real danger and frequent mis-use of this ability is to assume motives, usually wrong ones, on the part of others, particularly men. Only the Holy Spirit knows the spirit, which includes the motives, of a man.

Detail-orientation—This gift, when cultivated from a biblical perspective helps wives and moms to be wonderful home-makers. This skill, to use the common vernacular—"multi-tasking," is also necessary for being a capable administrator in a school setting, not to mention in other governments. From the Babylonian and Egyptian queens and empresses, to Debra, when surrounded by invertebrate males in Israel, to Britain's Queens Elizabeth I and Victoria, to Prime Minister Margaret Thatcher, to a goodly number of current women administrators in our sister schools, it has been historically proven that ABILITY is not a problem for women in administration. What is natural, i.e. juggling of details, for many women, has to be learned and consciously practiced by most men. So ability is not the only issue—we'll get to authority in a moment.

Steadfast, loyal, supportive—For all their gritty esprit de corps in combat situations, men don't hold a candle to the tenacious loyalty of women. Consider long-suffering Penelope of Odyssey fame. Twenty years she wept and pined for Odysseus, while he's out with the boys warring and whooping it up with goddesses. More biblically, consider that God commands women to respect their husbands, and men to love their wives. He commands to our weaknesses, not those areas He already made strong. Sadly, many women can love jerks of the first order who, the women admit, they can't imagine respecting.

Practical considerations for our purposes are looking to hire mature, home-making women, whenever possible, whose children are grown and/or in the school. They will stay and contribute their strength of steadfast support.

Feminine-nurture—It is no coincidence that professional nursing was begun by a woman, caring for wounded men in battle, Florence Nightingale, not to mention Clara Barton. Germane to our situations, it is a natural and good thing to have mostly women teaching and nurturing young elementary students, as is still typical. Nurturing is still very much part of what these young scholars need.

Gentlemen

Male characteristics, as God designed for marriage (and probably to restrain gender wars), complement female characteristics, when applied knowledgeably in our staffs.

Task-oriented (sometimes vs. people)—Without trying to read between the lines too much, I believe the Creation model is noteworthy for us. The Lord God could have made Adam and Eve at the same time, but He didn't. He first made Adam, then gave him a job, not a relationship. It was only after Adam noticed he, unlike all other creatures, was mateless, that God made Eve for Adam. (Of course, it was in His plan from the beginning.) Two things at least could be drawn from this: Men are designed for doing a job, and men need women at their sides to do that job. Not much has changed inherently from the garden. There's a reason more men than women die shortly after retirement. Both genders are to work and work hard, but whereas women frequently see relationships as the reason for their work (particularly in the home), men see work as separate from relationships. Keep that in mind as we get to boards.

Occasional cluelessness—Okay, so it's not just occasional. We really are clueless when it comes to details, relationships and group dynamics, that sort of thing. Any married woman knows this and at the same time this could be a news item for married guys. But there is more to life than details. I mention this here because it's real and, just as women should practice not assuming motives in the work place, men need to work at being detail-oriented. It matters that papers get graded on time and reports turned back in to administrators. Manners are love in the details, with social consequences. Male staffers must be gentlemen in our schools—demonstrating consideration to the ladies in details. Taking the time to notice and complement the ladies, who, unlike the guys, rarely combine plaids and stripes.

Big picture-visionary—The up-side of men missing details is that we delight in grand visions, philosophies, or maybe just a really big project. All the great philosophers we study in our schools were men. And without vision the people perish, the Word tells us. In educating children, our Father wisely gave men the responsibility and vision for generations, He gave women the ability to love children in countless particulars. Then, at least in part to keep us humble and relying on His strength, He commanded to our weaknesses; fathers are the ones responsible for the children's education and mothers are responsible to respect and follow their husbands' leading. We need each other.

Ready—shoot—aim—I don't like to think how many times Julie has saved me from my propensity to do just that. Particularly toward clueless male staff members or dads who don't get it! Given that historically men have been diplomats and ambassadors, it's not all that surprising the world has seen so many wars. In our schools, men can't be reminded too often that the students, particularly the girls, have feelings and families, all deeply affected by thoughtless words or actions. But at least some initiative is present in this characteristic, unlike the tendency to:

Avoid Responsibility vs. Take Responsibility—Taking the hit without excuses, which includes taking the initiative. Sadly many fledgling classical Christian schools are begun on paper by guys, but put into action by the ladies. Stick with it, gentlemen.

Masculine-strength—Though schools, as vehicles for educating children, appeal more naturally to the feminine side of the human race, we men are given the commands to educate. We have wimpy Christian schools, nationally, for the same reason we have wimpy churches—Christian men are currently, on the whole, wimpy. A strong school is not a military academy by definition; a strong school is a godly school with godly leadership and a God-centered vision. Looking over the gender options as to whose primary responsibility that is ... what is your final answer?

Differences between men and women were made by God, and therefore matter.

The study of and attention to these differences can enhance the joy and productivity of our school working environment—our second home in many cases.

My staff—We have a true kaleidoscope of personalities, an incredible collection of talented people, but fundamentally men and women of God. Below are some biblical standards that allow us to enjoy working together daily, weekly, monthly, yearly:

- Viewing things in the light of the morning—As I noted above, my wife has kept me from many major embarrassments by urging me to be slow to speak when I want to verbally guillotine someone. Have you noticed that frustrations, anxiety, and resentment are more frequent nocturnally? Wait for the morning to make hard, momentous decisions or actions when dealing with others in school. It'll at least give you time to phrase your speech more carefully, if not eliminate the need altogether.

- Keeping short accounts—Speaking of night and day, don't let the sun go down or the other person leave before you address any "awkwardness," differences, clashes, bumps, whatever you call breaking of fellowship. Stop sugar-coating sin and get right. Read and pass around *From Forgiven to Forgiving* by Jay Adams. I know of no better book for Christian-to-Christian collisions, which is particularly applicable to our situations.

- Joyfulness is not an option—Don't tolerate "cool professionalism" in your schools. You can't, nor should you try to be best friends with all of your colleagues. Neither should you expect them to all go bowling together every weekend, either. But there should be a thick atmosphere of general and genial pleasantness. "Good mornings!" and sincere smiles should abound; no dodging certain people or only communicating through business-like notes. Let me emphasize this in modern parlance—emails can be very helpful for some messages to other staff or parents, but limit them to information and quick replies. DON'T use them for trying to sort out inter-personal relationship concerns! Face-to-face is the best vehicle, even phone calls can be too impersonal and further the problem.
- Matthew 18—(Here it is again!) This should be as familiar to and practiced in our schools as the trivium. Speaking with crayon size letters—all concerns need to go first to the person who needs to know and is at the closest level to the issue. No "sparing her feelings," no "finding out what other parents think on this", in other words, no gossip! Confront in love and humility, or cover it with love. There are no other biblical options: cover or confront.
- Regular, solid nutrition from the Word and men of God—Another absolute standard for all staff: be in a solid church and be in it every Sunday you physically can make it. And never stop reading the Bible on your own. It'll be obvious, maybe only eventually, but obvious nonetheless if you (or anyone else) are not doing both. Summing up the standards for work biblically—be in joyful fellowship with God and

His saints or don't come to work. Righteousness: don't leave home without it.

General modus operandi

Some basic practical tips to help keep that oil of brotherhood pouring off Aaron's beard, as well as Miriam's flowing locks:

Communications:

It's critical so keep them frequent. They can be accomplished through verbal or written means, of course. Hand signals are not recommended for much. And then there are the inevitable, but potentially useful, meetings in person. The benefits of each mode, in relation to genders, are summed up succinctly below:

**Verbal:*

Women—Since the ladies are typically more diligent and attentive, the spoken word is usually adequate for brief communications.

Men—IF it's very brief, immediate, and concrete, verbal communications are okay. "Al, go move your car—the cement truck is about to back over it." Otherwise, write it down for the guys.

**Notes:*

Women—If the note is concise (vs. philosophical in nature), written in a clear, but pleasant manner, they are helpful. "Dear Betty, Just a quick reminder that our curriculum meeting is set for 3:15 today—like to have you there to contribute your thoughts!

Men—Notes are the best means to get some instructions across that involve more than two steps, provided you've trained them to look in their mailboxes more than once a leap year. But notes are a plus for all, and the note becomes an automatic written record of your more important communications. E-mails have come along since Logos started and they are extremely useful for both genders, as well as giving you a written record, assuming people have access to them and actually read them.

**Meetings:*

Women—They like the social aspects, but may lose focus regarding the objectives, so have a written agenda and let them plan the goodies to bring.

Men—They don't particularly like the social aspects, so have goodies with the agenda, (see how well that works?) but get it over with ASAP for the benefit of all concerned. They will respect you more for it and believe you understand the value of their time. And always remember goodies if it's going to be longer than about 45 minutes.

Appearances:

Professionalism, modesty, decorum—These are not options for the workplace. Modeling to the students is the passive aspect of thinking about our appearance; the other aspect is actively enforcing a standard of dress throughout the school. Astute women (alert to danger zones but not too prudish) can be a great aide to male administrators in this regard. A word fitly spoken to him in private regarding the blouse a young lady almost has on is very helpful and makes the administrator seem like he's able to notice details. Sober men can, with practice, tune in to less than appropriate dress and appearance among the guys and address it as men.

Encouragement, recognition:

Everyone needs an "atta boy" once in a while, women more than men, but the guys like it, too. Here again, notes are very easy, but this takes paying attention to each other a bit. The men will need more specific recognition than the ladies. Remember, we're built for accomplishing tasks and want to be noticed for doing a good job on them, not just a general positive comment about their persona.

Spiritual dimensions/jurisdiction: supporting covenantal authority:

Much could be said in this regard, since very few Christian schools really examine the scriptural principles applicable to Christian men and women in a workplace. They tend to do what it seems everyone else does, either emulating the squishy way many other Christian schools operate, or emulating the egalitarian way a worldly office complex operates. Let me point out two significant areas where bad patterns need to be avoided and godly ones reinforced:

Devotions vs. being devoted—When we come together as Christian adults in a Christian school, of all places, it does seem natural to focus in some way on the Lord, His Word, and His goodness. A typical response to this undeniable and appropriate desire is for staffs to have daily "devotions" of some sort together. Often the administrator feels a sense of responsibility to encourage his staff to greater heights of spirituality and so he may lead these devotions, sharing a portion of Scripture and what it means to him, and should probably mean to them, too.

Apart from the potential of having a poor handling of Scripture when everything is seen to apply to Christian schools, the administrator's fundamental thinking is just wrong. He has no biblical justification for leading his staff to "grow" or "worship" or any such thing. If anything, he may be doing more harm than good! For example, speaking at least for myself, I don't WANT another man, except my pastor, to attempt to spiritually lead my wife, in a Christian school or Safeway or anywhere else, unless I'm there, too. That's MY job, thank you very much!

As a Christian school administrator, I have a certain jurisdiction and authority over the men and women under me. That jurisdiction, particularly where it concerns the wives of other men, does not include their spiritual maturity. Covenantal authority, in the homes of the staff members as well as the families, needs to be acknowledged and honored. I can and should, if necessary, fire a female teacher for clear evidence of gross sin, but I can't and shouldn't take on the task of keeping her free from sin; that's her husband's (hence the title) job.

That being said, and strongly, there are other appropriate ways to acknowledge the Lord's presence when we come together as a Christian school staff. Briefly reading from, not instructing from, Scripture, may be appropriate, allowing the Word to speak for itself. We are commanded to sing with one another, a wonderful practice, even for the tune-impaired. And specific prayers for students and families (avoiding gossip) is always a good use of time since, again, we are commanded to pray without ceasing. Even a limited sharing of burdens before prayer can be constructive, if kept from become a counseling session. Above all, scriptural principles should be followed and the men should lead by example. Remember, you are gathering as Christians to do certain work; you are not gathering as believers in the formal act of worship and hearing the Word preached. You are a school, not the church.

Supporting biblical roles at the board level—Another significant area where Christian (and even classical) schools have been biblically stupid is how they construct and conduct their boards. Here again, worldly thinking abounds when it comes to what men and women should be doing. Imagine junior high, mixed genders in PE. Guys too rough, girls not being included, generally a lousy time being had by all. Now, take those same kids and problems 20 years into the future, at a board meeting, for instance.... Remember, the issue is authority, natures, and biblical roles, not ability! Qualified leadership—not sincere desires. Our culture and its rampant religion of egalitarianism (we are all really the same and deserve "equal" treatment) has had a devastating effect even on Christians. We have bought the lie and this thinking affects how we build and run our schools, unless we remember the antithesis and think biblically.

Remember, God's got it right, our culture's got it wrong. Never be embarrassed or apologize for what the Scriptures say about anything, particularly how men and women are to work and live together.

FREQUENTLY APPLIED PERSONNEL POLICIES

This a short list of policies that should be adopted:

- ASSIGNMENT OF PERSONNEL *CERTIFICATION
- ELEMENTARY JOB DESCRIPTION *COMPENSATION AND BENEFITS
- WORK AGREEMENTS (Contracts)
- PERSONAL LEAVE POLICY
- SEPARATION POLICY
- SUBSTITUTE TEACHERS
- CHURCH ATTENDANCE
- PUBLICATIONS POLICY
- ENROLLMENT OF STAFF CHILDREN
- HOME SCHOOLING OF STAFF CHILDREN

(The full version of these and other policies can be obtained from

Logos Materials. And now back to our regular program....)

A SHORT WORD ON VOLUNTEERS

In the beginning of any Christian school, there is a natural and welcome amount of enthusiastic offers of help, mostly from the parents. This is very good and should be carefully nurtured and guided by the administration. At the same time, there are some general principles that appear to apply to almost any situation involving volunteers. I would offer a few below.

*Volunteers should not (for long) be used to fill critical positions at the school, e.g. administrator, teacher, secretary, or even janitor. These positions should have clearly defined job descriptions, be under authority and be evaluated regularly, all aspects which are not typical of a volunteer's understanding or desires.

*Volunteers work best in roles that, while helpful to a teacher or administrator, do not require either long hours, daily attendance, or considerable responsibility. For those wishing to help on a regular basis, some tasks that fit the above criteria are:

- Recess duty
- Listening to reading groups
- Grading papers (at the lower levels)
- Bulletin board design
- Field trip chaperons
- Class party organizers
- Lunchroom, hall monitors

*Volunteers will always feel free to exercise the option of putting some event or task above the priority of being at the school. If that is not understood by all concerned, there will be friction and relationship problems very quickly.

*When seeking volunteer (unpaid) help for a large, one-time task, e.g. an auction or building playground equipment, you must be very organized to make the best use of their time and yours. A few tips on such a project:

- Give plenty of lead time and reminders.
- Be sure to personally ask the people you REALLY want there, then if you need more, put out a general call.
- Be sure to have all necessary materials ready to go on the day(s) of the project. No one likes to wait for other people to collect things or get prepared.
- Make sure the end is clearly foreseeable to all, i.e. you will all know when the job is done. For a building project, for instance, a clear goal and time frame for the work should be spelled out ahead of time.
- If the work will go over a meal time, either plan to pay for meals for everyone, or organize other volunteers to prepare a meal (good and lots of food!).
- Make the work as delightful as you can and you will likely win the volunteers over to help in the same way again.
- *NEVER assume a volunteer will be happy to keep doing the same work each year. Always ask and express appreciation frequently.
- *Finally, if you find that a volunteer is filling a critical role or a role that has become critical, offer to PAY the person. If that doesn't interest the person, make a job description and plan to replace that person as soon as you diplomatically are able. Remember, if your school needs it, figure out some way to PAY for it!

CHAPTER FIVE

Families

"Gate Keeping": Admission Matters

When I teach a painting elective class at Logos, I make a big point of telling the kids they may not use black paint in their paintings, especially when they are copying masters' works. And every year the students want to use it and I have to tell them that even though it may look like there is black in the work they are copying, it is highly unlikely the artist used it. Black pigment tends to dull every other color it mixes with, robbing the other color of its intensity and beauty. I tell the students that every square inch of their paintings should exude richness. Black flattens and dulls the portion of the canvas or paper it occupies. Okay, you get the idea that I don't think black paint is a good idea.

In somewhat the same way, choosing your students—and you need to realize you will have to choose students who enroll in your school—is like choosing the colors you will put on your palate. As with colors on a palate, your students will mix and blend, making up the canvas of your school's atmosphere. Therefore, you must be wise in your selections. (It should go without saying, but in our current culture I will spell it out:

the paint metaphor above was not in any way intended to be a racial reference. Okay? Sheesh.)

Few other decisions you make, or help make, will have greater, more profound ramifications for the entire work of the school. Choosing staff members pulls rank on this area, but not by much. The work of the teachers is enhanced or hindered by the composition of the student body. I mean these are the students we're going to teach, for goodness sake. So here are some thoughts to consider as you keep the gate to your school.

You Can't Be Two Mints In One!

If your school is still young (under five years), regardless of your school's name and motto, you will quickly discover that it is viewed by the public in one of two ways, generally.

Reform School—"Oh, you're a Christian school? Why then you must accept ALL kinds of kids, right?"

For good or ill, you will likely be asked by sincere parents to take on a wide range of behavioral problems with their children. Problems that would take an across-the-board revamping of your purposes and philosophy, not to mention some stalwart security personnel, to even start to address. You need to recognize these folks when they arrive in your office and before you enter into any agreement with them. There are a number of verbal clues that you can listen for, if the appearance of the student doesn't set off all sorts of alarms by itself. Here are some clues to listen for:

"We want to get junior away from a 'bad' group of friends."

Your mental response should be: "What would the parents of these 'bad' friends say about this kid?"

"We are going through some hard times at home and think it would be better to have junior in a Christian environment."

In other words, a divorce is likely imminent; treat this as you would if you were handed a live grenade—drop it quick and run for cover or you and those nearby stand a good chance of getting hit with the shrapnel. That may sound cruel or heartless, I realize. Fine, stick around and see what happens when the grenade goes off. You don't have to take my word for it. You won't be able to protect the child(ren), but you will probably find yourself (and your teachers) bleeding a bit for some reason.

"The teachers at his current school don't understand how to challenge and keep junior's interest."

While this may have some truth to it, your question should be, "And so how does junior, even though truly 'gifted,' spend his moments of boredom?" That would also be a good question to put to junior's current administrator.

"His father and I don't see the problems at junior's school the same way, but we're willing to give your school a try."

The parents don't agree on what is best for their child?! Right. So, if you take on the education of this child, you will be backing one parent as she (usually) tries to convince the other one of your school's worth. Yippee. And how much did you enjoy watching the Newly Wed Game? That was an insipidly stupid TV game show from the sixties wherein newly married couples made fools of each other and probably went on to play "The Newly Divorced Game." Stand by your standard, as much as it depends on you, of only accepting students from families where the parents do agree on the means of educating their children.

As I mentioned in an earlier chapter, a gentleman named Dr. Bob Smith came one day as a godsend to give us the good counsel that we could not be both a "reform" school and a good training ground for children being raised in the fear of God. We had already experienced the profound disappointment attending our "failure" to change problem kids into obedient kids. We had been firmly convinced that we could take all comers, good or bad. Then, with the sincere power of really neat Christian staff members surrounding and modeling for this kid, he would see the light and grow up to become the next George Muller. You can probably guess that we didn't see that happen real often.

Rather, surprise, we found the Scriptures rang true again on the point of "bad company corrupting good morals." God has so designed this world that it is much easier to destroy than build; a single match can reduce to ashes in a matter of hours a home that took years to complete. From hard experience we learned that one jerky kid can and will poison the air around him and many are defiled.

On the other hand, when we have expelled or just not re-enrolled certain students over the years, we have seen wonderful affects on the remaining classmates. Where there was a cloud of cynicism, rebellion, and disrespect hovering over the class, there is now the fresh breeze of joyful cooperation and cheerful obedience. We have cleared the blockage out of the pipe of godly influence from the home and the teachers. It really works and it is profoundly antithetical to the world's "wisdom," which would urge a Pollyanna, egalitarian view of human nature.

Training Camp—This is really the only other viable, desirable way you want your school to be viewed. That is, a place wherein you are building on a common foundation, already largely laid by the parents, so that you can work with them toward common goals. (This does not require them to be Christians—more on this later.) The Proverbs summation of "when they are old, they will not depart from it" states the job nicely. But this option necessitates a host of decisions, some of which will not win you the All-Around Sweet Guy Award.

Since in a large measure the students you enroll, and not you, will determine your "school spirit," are you going to just let it happen by default or you willing to plan for it? The bottom line here is: Are you willing to say "no" to a new or returning student/family, mean it, and take the consequences, come what may?

"Of course!" you say? Pause and think ... are you really willing to?

...Regardless of the budget demands breathing down your neck?

...Even if they're a family from your church?

...Even if they're a family which has been in the school for years, but their student has recently "gone south," so to speak?

...Even if it's a board member's rowdy child?

I trust the blood in your temples is pumping a bit harder at this point. Because if you're just mentally nodding assent to these questions, you don't really understand the stakes of the game. Saying "yes" is easy. But if you say "no" in some or all of those instances above, people will not LIKE you very much! And if your genetic orientation is like mine, that is, wanting to please all of the people all of the time, you will find yourself vainly seeking to have people understand why you had to make that awkward decision the way you did. Truly, truly I say unto you, they will rarely understand, much less agree with you. Stop trying to please at all costs. Ask God for a thicker skin and commit to do what's right.

ADMISSIONS: Philosophy First, Then Process

Before you let the first child into your school (if you have already, don't panic, just stay with me here), there are some basic questions that will define your philosophy of admissions:

- Who will be/is attracted to your school?
- Where will they come from?
- Which ones will you let in and try to educate?
- Will requiring the students to be Christians or come from a Christian home make your school climate and functioning all you want it to be?
- Will allowing non-Christians in your school adversely affect your school climate and functioning?
- How many non-Christians is too many?
- What do you want, anyway?

Two most common Christian School philosophies on admissions

"Discipleship"—That is, the school is building on an assumed common, biblical foundation, reflected in admission requirements. Many, if not most, non-denominational Christian schools make this assumption, typically accompanied by "requiring" believer status of the student and/or the parents. This approach is also frequently taken by many staunchly Reformed brothers who believe they must allow ONLY clearly Reformed/Calvinistic families in their schools. This fulfills the family's and church's covenantal responsibility to train children up in the faith, as they see it. Inherent admission problems abound with this severe approach, the most obvious being, who gets to determine, and how, the true believer status of these families? How accurate a reflection of a heart's status is a signed profession?

"Open Enrollment"—Here, whether or not the student is a Christian, the school takes on an evangelistic purpose, and thereby assumes authority of some sort over the child's spiritual status and sanctification.

Many Christian schools dating from the sixties, begun as a reaction to the Supreme Court's anti-prayer, anti-Bible rulings, use this philosophy. They were founded often on reactionary themes, with no clear thought as to an overarching purpose or educational philosophy. If they were ice cream, they would be vanilla. Therefore, by default (and their fault), they have adopted many public school approaches, the worst being that they have assumed authority, especially spiritual, over the kids, just by being a Christian school. Pathetic programs and materials are tried each year to bolster the students' characters and spiritual understanding. Parental authority is still negated. The results should be painfully obvious. Many, many of the graduates of these schools also "graduate" from Christianity.

A Third Option—"Covenant Support"

Roughly defined, this is the view that God made families, all families, and His commands regarding educating children are to fathers and mothers, not schools. Sounds obvious doesn't it? But it has some rather profound applications for us. Note: This philosophy of admissions acknowledges, and encourages the biblical role and authority of even non-biblical homes. It puts the emphasis on defining what the school is and is not, and what it can and cannot offer. It is truth in advertising—"let the buyer beware." Before we look at the details of the process, what does this covenantal option offer? (And you don't have to be Reformed to offer it—we weren't and still aren't as a school.)

Benefits and biblical support of a "Covenantal" approach to admissions

It reflects reality—The unsaved will make it into your school no matter what. Everyone, saved and unsaved, knows that even the "best" churches have non-believers attending week after week for a variety of reasons. How much more true will that be for a Christian school whose purpose is academic training, not specifically worship? (Although there should be a recognized connection.) The unsaved WILL be there—let's be honest and see the world as it is.

It encourages emphasis on contrasts in living for the redeemed vs. the lost. Neither Christ nor Paul in their teachings on the New Covenant and its applications ever said "Here is the sure-fire litmus (doctrinal) test you are to use to determine whether or not someone else's name is in the

Book of Life." Rather, the clear emphasis in Christ's teaching is judging the quality and presence of FRUIT, not the stuck-on label. Fruit, as defined in Scripture, is evidenced in living, not signed documents or verbal assents. Quality living takes time to evaluate, just like fruit takes time to mature ("He who endures to the end will be saved"). In our schools we live together many hours each day through the year—the fruit will eventually be seen.

It reduces the potential for encouraging spiritual hypocrisy. Such as the assumption, "We're all headed to heaven!," which can be the attitude within many Christian schools. Talk about dangerous presumptions, with a belittling of the true Gospel! Jesus had hard words, not for the obvious sinners who were wretched in their sin, but for the "healthy" who didn't "need" a doctor. Kids, especially older ones, are pretty good at being chameleons (assuming the coloring of their background to fit in or hide). How easy do we make it for them to assume the coloring of sanctification if in our teaching, casual talk and school policy we act as though every child is right with God and on a fast track to heaven's eternal bliss? It is certainly understandable that we want to assume these little ones we love are in the kingdom already. They may be and likely are, but we don't want to fall into dangerous covenantal presumptions through "requiring" a testimony or signed statement. It just isn't our call to make.

It reduces a works-righteousness mentality. A favorite here is that having the kids do community projects = godly testimony to the community. There is nothing wrong with community projects and they do say something about our school. But it's the same thing that can be said about the college fraternity that does the same project. It is not a means or an evidence of our students' sanctification, nor is it a "witness" to the community of Christ's gospel, which is often the reason given for doing these things. Of course we can and should encourage and even admonish the students who claim Christ as Lord (e.g. in assemblies, prayer times, singing, etc.), but we (schools) are not administering sacraments. That's the Church's job.

It actually puts greater responsibility on the staff living righteously as examples and in enforcing godly standards by all in the school, not just the principal or in-house pastor. Speaking of fruit, outside the school we (the staff) are viewed collectively by the community, inside the school we are individuals to the kids. Our "guard," i.e. conscious lives before God, must be up at all times knowing we are likely modeling Christ before unsaved students. We must not "let down" as we may be tempted to at home or among fellow believers at church. (Not that "letting down" is ever really an option—it tends to let in what is known as "sin.")

Very significantly, this view reinforces the biblical role of family/parents in the God-ordained triad: Family, Church, State. God established the realms of jurisdiction, not man. There are always problems when those biblical boundaries are violated, even with the best of intentions and sincerity. We know the State's problems; can we spot our own usurping of parental authority in the Christian school world? We do not have school counselors who address the emotional, spiritual needs of our students. Even for the unsaved students, the parents (and their church, if part of the picture) of the student must be honored and deferred to in any significant discipline issue at school, how much more for an issue as eternal as the student's salvation? We must know our place and pray.

It also reinforces the biblical concept of being in the world, not of it, as well as having "strangers" in our midst. God chose His people Israel for His own purposes, not because they deserved it or had any special genetic attractiveness. As such, they were to be holy (set apart) and yet still have dealings with "the stranger and alien in their midst." Nothing's changed in that regard for His people. On earth we will have strangers among us, some we will recognize as such, and like the Israelites we are to treat them kindly and not exclude them (except from worship). Others will be far more insidious strangers, those who call themselves by the Name but despise it by how they live. So who might have the worst affect on our schools again?

This view allows for non-Christians to 'inhale' the "fragrance of life" by being around Christians. Even though our primary purpose is pursuing a biblical paedeia, i.e. a godly enculturation of the students, as we set upon this task, by God's grace, the gospel will do its work among our students. Some students will indeed be drawn to the sweet smell of abundant and true life, even while others may be repelled by it.

Finally, it offers less potential for Christian cheesiness and kitsch, while it encourages more applied biblical thought. In modern evangelicalism, reflected in the "all togetherness" of Christian schools, there is way too much emphasis on outward adornment, vs. inward (working out) reality. So Christian kitsch (posters, games, music, talk) is easy when no one challenges it; sort of like Christian cheerleading. Whereas, recognizing that families do indeed come from all sorts of backgrounds, including churches of every flavor, our schools can and should pursue biblical reasoning through discussion and training.

Now, to the Admissions Process...

The process should be geared for enrolling families that are a "best fit" vs "first-come, first-served." So, in your published applications and handbooks clearly describe what your school values and encourages, then let the families determine if that's what they want to commit to. Your mission statement, philosophy and goals should be the starting point for educating interested families. And these can't be clearly stated unless they are clearly thought through first by your school:

- They should be expressed in broad terms since particulars will change from year to year, even grade to grade. The mission should be a long-term view, a vision with enough teeth to give strength and durability to school over time, but not so many teeth that it needs constant oral surgery to be current.
- The goals should be clearly stated in Admission procedures/documents to help ensure families come in with their "eyes open," i.e. they have a pretty good idea what the school is about, even before they sit down with you.

First Interview: (Probably not the first time you meet them. Set another time to sit down together.)

If possible, get a view of both parents, present or absent, since both will influence the life of the student. At Logos, our standard is that if one of the parents is fundamentally opposed to the students being there, even if the parent is a divorced, absent parent, we will likely not accept the students. We will not get into the middle of a familial civil war.

No one wins in those situations, and there is a good chance the battle ground will extend into the school. Require both parents to come to the interview, if at all physically possible, and let them both know how important their involvement is in the school, but more particularly in the schoolwork of their child.

Review the basics of your school ("Have you had a chance to read our handbook?"), allow for questions, (you may have to supply some, e.g. "Many parents ask about our discipline policy and practices....") But the ONE question you must get an answer to, regardless of who asks it is: "WHY do you want your child at our school?" Another way of putting it, is "What led you to seek enrolling your child here?" But I personally like the first one best. Cover as much territory during this time as possible, including financial arrangements and any possible entrance testing that may be necessary. If they are coming from a homeschool situation, there are a host of possible questions that can come up. (I have written a small article called *Homeschool to Classical School***.)

During the interview with the parents and the student, you need to determine their purposes and understandings in seeking enrollment. I would love to tell you that every set of parents has only Ephesians 6 in mind when they come to your school. But you wouldn't believe me anyway. So, on this point, that is, the parents' understandings, here is my patent-pending, suggested range (grades F-A) representing the mental (not written) grading scale you may want to consider with families: (Based loosely on their level of commitment and understanding of what your school offers.)

F Level Understanding—"Government schools have their problems but, hey, at least it's the American, democratic way. We're just checking your school out as a alternative." (Don't hold your breath waiting for them to come back.)

D Level Understanding-"Our kids can and should be 'salt & light' in the public schools since there are so many witnessing opportunities. We hope your school can help us prepare our kids to go there (or back there) someday." (Probably most common among modern Christians.)

C Level Understanding—"OK, our kids may not be saving souls in the

** Read at logosschool.com/another-classical-education-article/

public schools, but they are at least surviving without any big problems. We hear you may have a better academic and discipline program for our child." (More realistic, but could jump ship if pushed a bit, such as the work being too difficult.)

B Level Understanding—"Enough's enough! Homeschooling (or the government school) hasn't worked out like we thought it would. We want our kids in a Christian school. Yours has a good reputation and we have friends who have their kids here." (They may go either way. Once they forget how bad "Egypt" was they may have no problem returning to whatever. Or they might grow in understanding and commitment to the classical, Christian philosophy and commit to it. Time will tell.)

A Level Understanding—"We have prayed and thought long and hard about this. We believe it's our responsibility to train up our kids with a biblical worldview. After considering what your school offers, particularly the rigorous, but supportive classical, Christian instruction, as well as hearing good things from others...." (No, really, you might actually get some families like that! Granted, they're primo and rare, unless you have a great church locally. By that I mean one with a pastor dedicated to Christian education.)

NOTE: Even non-Christian families could be up to B Level and many times are. At the same time, many Christian families you know stay at the D Level, sad to say.

Other Considerations

Siblings can tell you a lot about how the student you're considering has been trained. Watch how mom and dad respond (or not) when the three-year-old brother of the applicant starts climbing your bookshelves. I have a bust of Theodore Roosevelt in my office. One little litmus test I have used for the family is whether or not their precocious toddler threatens TR; if so, we're done. I have actually had younger siblings come around to my side of the desk and clamber past me to play with my computer keyboard, without so much as a peep from mom or dad.

Past schools, even government schools, should be queried, especially in the case of a dubious decision. I have found that what is written in a permanent record and what you may be told "off the record" on the phone are often at opposite ends of the dial. Candid, unrecorded comments are often the most revealing. To vary Scripture a bit, "even a stinker of a child is known by his deeds, whether in a government school or a Christian school." And very rarely do the people in the know want to tell Mom and Dad the truth, so they don't.

Character matters far more than a high GPA. More specifically, the student (especially older ones) should display an eager willingness to learn and work. Again, the interview and documentation up front can tell you a lot about a student's work habits or aptitude. But the reaction of the student and parents to actual exposure to your classrooms will elicit a telling response from them. They will, most likely, be overwhelmed, but eager to plunge in, or overwhelmed and hesitant. ("Overwhelmed" should be the common element. If a student can come from another program and fit very easily into your school, you might not be doing all you should or could be doing. Just a tip to the wise.) Evidence of fear of the amount and/or level of work at your school should be taken seriously by you.

Academic potential considerations: You knew we had to get around to this sooner or later, so here it is. Contrary to popular opinions about (or against) Christian schools, we don't just take "the best and the brightest" kids. At the same time, you can't make a good omelet with rotten eggs. Or, to quote C.S. Lewis, sort of: You can pour a lot of fine wine into a mud puddle, but you still end up with a mud puddle. So, since we are in the business of educating students in a rather rigorous program, it is very necessary to determine if they have the prerequisite equipment.

Even neat kids from great families may not have the background and requisite skills to make it in the grade the family put on the application. You will need some objective measuring tools to assist you and the parents in putting the student where he has the best chance of succeeding. After many years of too many frustrating bad fits, (often based on previous school's worthless report cards) we finally designed our own entry/placement tests. Each spring the elementary teachers check and modify the tests in math, grammar, writing, and reading skills to accurately reflect the requisite levels for passing their grade. Then the tests are given to their students to determine the average score. These tests are administered to all new student applicants, usually in the spring, immediately following the end of the school year. (We try to arrange to have the majority of the testing done in one pre-set day and ask the applicants to come to the school for that purpose.) This has been very helpful in starting the students off well, at the level they are best prepared for.

Published expectations/requirements are also very helpful to the parents. You can't put your whole curriculum guide in the student-parent handbooks, but you can describe enough that the parents know what they are up against in each discipline and at each grade, generally. This should be true even of kindergarten. The distance between where current educational expectations are and where your school's are heading will widen, just like a ship pulling away from the pier. Even your sincerest, most convinced families may be still standing on the pier and they need to know how far they'll have to jump to avoid getting soaked. (Okay, it's a lame analogy, but you get the picture.)

A good rule of thumb: As much as possible design your application and acceptance/rejection process to avoid the appearance of personal, subjective decisions—"I'm not accepting your kid because I don't like his face."

We like "Test Drives" for secondary student, especially. That is, arrange for a school/class visit by the student. It lets you observe the student, while he is observing the school (more likely he is checking out what your kids are like).

Acceptance—Hurray!

Should the student be accepted by you, an Acceptance letter should be sent pronto. It should include the date the school year starts (if summer time), name(s) of the child's teacher(s) and tips for a smooth transition, especially into the secondary program (7-12). You may want to attach a supply list, a calendar, and class list of students. You should also have a well thought-out plan of events to help new families become familiar and comfortable with the school as soon as possible. Information always goes better with food, don't forget!

Good Admissions Takes Discernment... What Doesn't?

Consider this, the lack of or loss of biblical acuity in your school is frankly not the fault of who we let in, but rather of those who let them in! So ... are you worried about getting too many unbelievers? Bad influences? It won't be the kids' fault:

*Who was asleep at the switch? Why did the school drop its gate-keeping guard?

*Know what kind of climate (morale, culture) and function you want, then require it! Maintenance is living, working, deciding well.

But there are other issues to Admissions, such as bringing families up to speed (if they have, as most families do, more than one child, you want them to stay, but also grow in their understanding and commitment).

Enrolling & Educating PARENTS

You never just enroll just a STUDENT, you always enroll a FAMILY. Further, each child is affected by many folks, not just Dad and Mom, most of whom you won't meet. It's sort of like when you got married: you picked your spouse, but you didn't know all the in-laws you were also marrying into. Okay, perhaps it's not as daunting as that, but similar in impact.

Obviously the child's parents and siblings are the people most affected by what that child undergoes at school, so it is those people you need to consider primarily in your communications. Most importantly, God's Word demonstrates His view of the covenantal home as an organic unit, not a collection of autonomous individuals. Did you ever hear or read the post-modern definition of a family? "A family is a circle of friends who love you!" Mercy!

But since God made and defines the family, our culture may as well try redefining water for all the affect they will ultimately have. From the Old Testament to the New Testament, God brings many blessings and curses on to families, with the exception of direct judgment for individual sin.

One of the dictums in the economic world is that you get less of what you tax and more of what you subsidize. This can have a positive side—if you know and apply the biblical standards for regarding families, when you insist on getting to meet both parents (as possible), when you refer discipline problems to dads (not moms), when you refuse to enroll or when you expel students of parents who don't share the school's convictions of child rearing, then you are subsidizing one view. This will result in the blessing of getting more of those families you want, and not getting or keeping families you don't want. Yes, there are indeed families you don't want.

If that is an unwelcome idea then your school will not know the blessings I am speaking of, to say the least.

By having more and more of the families who share your convictions you will find that your school goals will be fleshed out in the lives of your graduates in an increasingly satisfying manner.

The enrollment process is just the first step in educating the parents (not just the student)

It begins with the application—How much can you request and inform in the document? We took a cue from a sister school and increased the number and scope of our probing, personal questions about the family's goals and priorities. It became a much larger application but much more informative to both sides than before. Remember, it's much easier to turn back at that point than it is further down the road. Broken engagements are tough; broken marriages are horrible.

The first year matters—a lot! (This is the Honeymoon period.) Many positive experiences and communications should build a solid relationship. But remember your goal is to move the parents from the most common level of understanding, "B Level," (remember the range above?) to a good, solid A! So don't include just warm fuzzies—pass along lots of specific information and education on WHY this is so good. Such as:

Newsletters/student paper—School news, yes, but more insights need to be communicated than just what is happening, e.g. addressing the WHY of classical, Christian ed.

Books—There are loads more now than there were in 1981 (when we opened). Purchase a caseload or two and give a copy to all your families. We have received many positive, encouraging comments in response to our give-aways. (Make sure your staff gets a copy, too.)

Speakers—This is harder to do and more expensive, but frequently worthwhile. Try to make an evening of it and have the kids present something and offer food, the parents will come. But don't just push your own speakers, encourage attendance at good speakers wherever they are: other churches, universities (debates, seminars) if they are addressing the WHYs.

ACCS communications/activities—It can be very encouraging and enlightening to the parents to know that there are OTHERS out there with the same convictions and goals for their kids, an increasing amount!

Staff-parent communication/reports—Your staff members need to understand and be able to communicate, in simple terms, the uniqueness of what you are doing. True, a certain saturation point is necessary, which requires time on task for them. Another reason for thorough and basic staff training.

Communicating the vision in practice. This is, of course, the meat-and-potatoes of bringing your parents along. The good and appropriate rhetoric you put forth must be backed up by years of nuts-and-bolts teaching and learning in the classrooms which speaks volumes to your families. This includes:

- The daily class work, with all its messages, both directly and indirectly, which tell the child he's loved. The parents can see the teacher's nurturing, as well as the practical progress the child makes in meeting curriculum goals.
- School spirit plays a large role in how quickly and well a student "fits in" and feels secure. This includes the natural student-student interaction. Distinctives of your school's atmosphere will become clear to the families as will the kinds and natures of friends in school.
- Parent-parent interaction, in classes, assemblies, games, Christmas programs, field trips will also be an important way families learn more about the school and the reality of its vision. No regulation by you will be necessary or even possible; it will just happen, but your daily integrity in dealing with parental concerns, rumors, and questions will help this

activity be productive. Parents can and will reassure other parents about the leadership of the school.

- School programs will also instruct parents about the vision, positively or negatively, depending on whether your programs match your vision or they just happen as they always have. There should be increasing quality, not relying on the cuteness factor to carry the day.

Educating parents is an unceasing task—each succeeding family needs to know

Don't grow weary—plan freshly for it!

You can't assume everyone or even long-term families are at the A level. Keep preaching and doing the same message, i.e. fleshing out your clear vision year after year after year. But keep it fresh before your eyes and heart, so that you can freshly communicate it to every family in your school. Results will be evident in the long-run, don't settle for first return flushes of excitement. Like our sanctification—he who endures to the end will see and enjoy the greatest blessings! One blessing we have enjoyed is seeing the school improve through the support and involvement of more and more convinced, committed families.

A Scary Side to Parental Communications: MOTHER BEARS

"Let a man meet a bear robbed of her cubs, rather than a fool in his folly." -Prov. 17:12

Scripture makes it clear that there are indeed worse things than coming face-to-teeth with a mama grizzly who thinks you've been messing with her kids. But keep in mind it is a relative comparison, as you see in the above quote. In fact, the relative undesirability of being in company with a fool is quite heightened by the comparison, in my opinion. True, I have never actually had the occasion to be any closer to a bear than when he's been safely behind the bars of a zoo, but I have read too many of those Drama In Real Life Stories in *Reader's Digest*; "...his teeth were as big as railroad spikes, crushing my head with the power of a hundred vises! I knew I was going to die!"

If I ever had had the desire to backpack in the wilds of Yellowstone Park, those stories would have cured that impulse very quickly. In fact, I take walks near our home only during the day.

Nevertheless, in my own little way, I believe I have had more than one encounter with "mother bears" right here in Logos School. My tangles have left only a few mental and emotional scars on my psyche, but they haven't been real pretty sights, either. Hackles raised, blazing eyes boring into mine, claws at the ready, growls barely restrained under the surface of her strained voice, mothers of not a few students over the years have held me at bay. Under my calm demeanor, sweat glands and heart were at maximum pumping power, and I mentally thanked Providence that a rather hefty desk was between me and certain destruction. Lacking any real firepower at hand, I have had to rely only on my own wits and the power of calming rhetoric:

"Now, Betty, I understand exactly how you feel, but you have to see it from my side, too. If you kill me now, my own four children will be really disappointed! You do see that, don't you?" I have also discovered that my rhetoric can be enhanced by my kneeling behind my desk.

How do these situations come about? I frequently ask myself that same question. In fact it often comes to mind when I find myself kneeling behind my desk, pleading for my life. Actually, these situations, unlike a real bear hunting trip, often spring upon me without much warning at all. I mean, when one heads into the woods, with some anticipation, and better yet, some preparation for such an encounter, then the bear arriving on the scene should cause little more surprise than seeing another actor come on stage at his cue. "Oh, there you are," the hunter might even say, "It's about time! I was beginning to wonder if I had the right forest."

But I don't get such deliberate anticipation or planning. No, usually the first I know of these life-threatening experiences is when my office door bursts open, and hovering over me is a seething mother, often with semi-crumpled school papers in her paw, er, her fist. Then, if I am lucky, instead of instantly shredding my sensitive emotions with her razor-sharp remarks and accusations, she holds herself in check and asks if I have a "few minutes" for her to ask me some questions. Often those situations can hold out the hope that life may go on and we can come to some reconciliation.

However, appearances can be deceiving and, though outwardly calm with me, she may have committed some blood-letting before she got to my door. I have had occasions when I thought we had separated with all my parts still functioning as they should, only to find, upon tracing the mother's tracks through the school building, a teacher bleeding profusely from multiple wounds. The teacher is not really close to death, she just has the look of a wife at the site of a mining accident: barely holding herself together, and obviously suffering from shock and disbelief. So we work through it—her telling me that after twelve years of teaching she now realizes that she is a total failure and should take up garbage-collecting; me telling her that she is not a failure and that Logos, yay verily, the entire Christian school movement in the United States of America needs her to stay in teaching.

Godly perspective, as always, is the key to these situations. The "mother bear" moms usually calm down and come to see that we are truly sorry for causing mental anguish for her cubs, er, kids. And we usually come to see that we may have been hasty in assigning blame, or too many homework pages, or whatever. Dads, like softening music when present, can play a key role in providing that calming effect on upset moms:

"Martha, you heard Mr. Garfield say he will review the test with Mrs. Johanson. OK? Now, let's go home and let him come down off the bookshelf."

Note: Obviously I used some facetiousness in the article above, but there is also a fair bit of truth to it. Another recent and related phenomenon has been developing that I wanted to give you a "heads-up" about. That is working with single parents, in the vast majority of cases, single moms. Divorce is with us to stay, very likely, even in our Christian contexts. Here are a few observations on the topic that I've made over the years:

- You will likely have an increasing number of single moms seeking to enroll their children.

- They very often have financial burdens you will need to consider and address.

The "absent" fathers may be in a variety of situations:

- Moved away
- Re-married
- Hostile to having their kids in your school
- Hostile to former wife, and to anyone taking "her" side (!)
- Living locally
- Wanting to receive school reports about their kids
- Almost any combination of the above, and more (we have had two widows, so far)

The mom may be doing a tremendous job of raising her kids alone.

The mom may LOOK like she's doing a great job, but is actually a pressure-cooker on high heat.

It takes two to tango, and to tangle—rather rarely was the husband the only one at fault in the marriage. If her issues were not dealt with biblically before she came to your school (i.e. repentance, forgiveness, bitterness left behind, etc.), well, I'll just say—WATCH OUT!

Get a copy of any divorce/custody agreement. You will possibly need it to know what the story is. Don't flinch at this—you are getting involved in this family's life, for better or worse, so to speak. You need details that might affect the students' lives.

We have had all types of single moms here. Most have been a joy to work with. Others have caused some of our worst nightmares ... really. Pray for wisdom and ask lots of questions before you admit their students. Oh yes, and make sure they sign a document that says they "agree and will comply with all your school's policies."

He's Not Your Child: Respecting Parents' Roles

According to statistics I read somewhere, the divorce rate among self-avowed Christians in the US is the same as for the pagans, i.e. about 50%. Further, in almost every other aspect related to the implosion of a family, the similarities far outweigh the differences between pagan and Christian. So what do we see in our schools when families we loved and served self-destruct? Bitterness, tears, accusations back and forth, the child caught in the middle—devastated or withdrawn, grades and work quality go in the toilet, and general, all around disruption.

And all through it we frequently hear the stupid, pathetically limp reassurances from one or more parent, such as—"This is hard on all of us, but the Lord has been good and we think the kids are going to be fine. This will be better for them. We will just have to adjust but it'll be okay." Yuck.

It's not a matter of who does know best—who's in charge...

If you stay in Christian ed, even classical, long enough, you will see a child you love suffer in some form (not necessarily from actual physical abuse) at the hands of their own parents. What do you do? The very understandable temptation is to step up to bat for the child, and maybe wish to use the bat on a few assorted adults' heads. Understandable. And altogether wrong. Not just because it would make a mess of a perfectly good bat, but because even if you were able to be an articulate defender of the child, God has so designed the world that the home is the greatest influence on a young child's life, regardless of how many "waking hours" a child spends in school.

I have had to expel a second grade lad. Why? With all our godly resources, modeling and love, he was following his parents' example of behavior, i.e. bad!

Let's stack the temptation deck higher ... is it possible for *you* to know more about what the child needs than the parents do? YES. Especially if the parents are in sin, you may be more spiritually and even practically knowledgeable to address that child's needs. So what? I have seen many husbands verbally and emotionally mistreat their wives—that doesn't qualify me to step in and assume the husband's role.

Note: I am purposely not getting into the realm of offering good counsel, either from yourself or encouraging them to seek more qualified counselors. That is totally legitimate, but from my experience, that is very rarely appropriately offered, and even more rarely acted upon, in the school setting. Advice unsought for is a waste of everyone's time and breath.

Reader's Digest grace

God's grace is often as mysterious as it is deep. I have read my share of feel-good stories in *Reader's Digest* about the teacher/principal whose loving, patient influence profoundly affected a child's life for good, in spite of the child being brought up in the ghetto, never knowing their parents, etc., and they go on to win the Nobel Peace Prize. I'm really not trying to be facetious, but far too many Christians think that they're a Protestant version of Mother Theresa, or at least they should try to be. According to Scripture, God's PRIMARY means of saving and sanctifying grace to children is through the parents.

An attending, almost unavoidable, consequence of a hurting child in your school/class is the temptation to give him a disproportionate amount of attention. This is anything but appropriate. Let me be as plain as I can: if you have a class of 20 students and one little guy is suffering through a home on the rocks, if the students see you spending loads of love and time on him, what is the message they are getting? Problems at home = lots of nice attention from teacher. Whoops.

Further, an older child's behavior may rapidly deteriorate during a family crisis. Here the temptation is to lighten up and cut him some slack. His parents may even ask for this. This again is dead wrong and is breaking faith with the other students and parents in the class.

The Biblical pattern of familial roles (Remember, these apply to ALL families, regardless of their recognition of God's authority or not; it's simply how He made the world!)

Fathers—The covenant (contractual) head, he has final responsibility for everything that comprises and affects the family life; he is to love and nurture his wife, provide for all the family's creature needs, including spiritual, and comforts (seasoned to taste) for all in the home. He is lawgiver, top educator, advocate, prosecutor for children—king and servant in his own castle.

Mother—The queen, the cherished and respected executive officer, yet servant of all; the cheerleader for her husband and kids; nurse, top designer for the home; communications expert between home and school; the family billboards her tastes and standards of cleanliness, just as they exhibit Dad's standards in behavior.

Children—Beloved peasants, heirs to a throne at the right time; servants to all—each other and especially parents; recipients of the family heritage (for good or ill); designed to learn and copy patterns for life and marriage. But since they are, so to speak, our bread and butter, let's take a moment or so to consider how we see them through our particular vision....

STUDENTS—How do they look in a classical school context? (News item: Boys and girls are different!)

Grammar level: (Pre-Polly and Poll-Parrot)

Little girls—Wide-eyed, wonder-filled, ready to believe anything the lovely teacher says, notice details of color, design, pattern, love the chants, the reciting, the songs—all thrills of the grammar stage; generally they are more in tune with the great work of school then the boys, they thrive on order and schedules, then they go home to teach school to their younger siblings, dolls, or the family dog (not many boys do that!).

Young lads—Wide-eyed also, but attracted to (as well as easily distracted by) the tangibles, touching and tasting, making sounds, building, cutting, coloring (vigorously); possibly a bit more skeptical of teacher's pronouncements than the girls, enjoy the work (the physical, productive side) vs. the talking, remember the tangibles, so will need more repetition than the girls; overall, higher energy content with less self-control, at least initially (hence the ADHD head hunters capture the guys in droves).

Logic/Dialectic: (Pert)—Dramatic changes, equated with on-set of puberty (Remember those days?)

Young ladies—Image becomes important, both their own and their work, want precision in directions/ instructions, but still rather gullible—less argumentative than guys, sincere, need protection from fallacy of ad hominem (verbal attacks "to the man" vs. the point) so debates need structure, much more likable than guys at this point, they still can be openly excited by school.

Young gentlemen—"Pert" thy name is "junior high boy," especially in a debate (formal or informal), may resist or not want to face the changes he's going through (Peter Pan syndrome), but likes the rough and tumble of issue arguments, rather clueless about what young ladies are like and need, e.g. courtesy and gentleness, still likes the physical side of things, e.g. the visible aspects of learning—models, diaramas, maps, etc., especially if he gets to explain their significance to others.

Rhetoric (Poetic): For our purposes, it seems this is the shortest stage we can see. Poll-parrot goes into high gear in third grade and usually lasts until about sixth grade, then fades into Pert which doesn't fade, especially in guys, until they're about forty-five. Okay, actually about late ninth, but more likely early tenth grade (guys really are frequently behind the curve here, too). So we get to see Poetic traits for only about two or so years, typically.

Ladies—The somewhat awkward or gangly, albeit endearing, little gosling has now become quite the swan. We especially notice this in our Protocol events. In our "lower protocol" (ninth and tenth grades), the girls are precious and cute, but don't always seem to know how to carry themselves. By "higher protocol," they are graceful and even elegant. In the classrooms they are confident, curious, and well-spoken. They are still very eager to please their teachers and may go overboard on hard assignments. The "bigger" picture, philosophically and historically, is clearer to them now and they can write and speak from that vantage.

Gentlemen—Those that have most benefited from the long-haul (gone through the earlier stages in your school) will also be rather confident and well-spoken. Writing may still be somewhat harder to do well and will usually be much more concise than the ladies'. They want to be respected and, if given the opportunity, will take a serious attitude toward serious leadership. Their particular interests (humanities, sciences) now are evident and they want to pursue them further, but don't have a lot of patience with other ("uninteresting") material. While school overall may not seem to thrill them, they like the order and work, as well as specific teachers and coaches. They really do like to be there (and if there are some nice girls there, too, that doesn't hurt).

NOTE: The students I've described above may sound somewhat idealized. They are not. I could easily think of faces and names as I wrote this and they were not a small minority. "Teen-agers" (what a dumb name!) don't have to be walking/talking embarrassments to all who know them. One of the real benefits of the classical, Christian vision is the cultural reformation that can and should occur in our schools. Etiquette, for instance, is just love in the details of living life together. Guys holding doors and waiting for young ladies should be the norm, not the odd kid. How your oldest kids look and act will and should speak volumes about the entire education you are providing. Of course it's a given that your families will have the greater impact, but all the more reason to help certain families to "come along" with your upgrade toward a delightful, biblical view of all life, even in school.

GENDER "EQUALITY" IN EDUCATION? AN OXYMORON IN ACTION

"What are little girls made of? Sugar and spice and everything nice, That's what little girls are made of."

"What are little boys made of ?

Frogs and snails and puppy dogs' tails, That's what little boys are made of."

God, in His limitless wisdom, has created boys and girls to be different since Time began. Countless cultures and centuries have confirmed this fact; it is only in the latter part of the twentieth century, in a remote corner of the globe, that parents are being sold the ridiculous notion that their sons and daughters are exactly alike, really. It would be humorous except for the fact that parents are buying it and becoming frustrated, even abusive, when their children insist on displaying behaviors once considered "typical" for boys or girls.

This "sameness doctrine" is especially evident in the expectations placed on children entering school. Little girls in kindergarten are frequently encouraged to play with traditionally male-type toys (trucks, cars, bugs), while little boys in the class are encouraged to check out the toy stoves and dolls. Why isn't Johnny playing house?

It continues on through the remainder of their educational career. It may become less overt, but actually far more detrimental. If Johnny can't read as soon as Sally, then, of course, it means he is probably learning-disabled and needs special education. Jane is having trouble with math and doesn't seem to have any interest in science. Let's change the curriculum or maybe just send in the "specialists," the high priests of the new religion of Egalitarianism, the mantra of which is "All must receive the same or equal rights." Amen. Yes, there are students with real problems who need extra help. But have you ever stopped to wonder why, with all our culture's other advances, it is in this generation we have the lowest proportion of readers and the largest special education bureaucracy in educational history? Could it have something to do with how the children are taught, and not a problem with the children themselves?

Historically, in almost every culture, only boys received a formal education. Then, in the western cultures within the last couple of centuries, all-girl schools began to pop up (frequently as a result of Christians wanting to raise their daughters to be intelligent, articulate wives and mothers!). Separate schools were the norm for quite some time. Relatively speaking, "co-ed" schools are a new invention. Why were schools so long "gender specific"? The simplest and most obvious answer is that, until recent history, people recognized the fact that girls and boys act, learn, and even think differently.

Ever since Dewey (possibly even Mann), the theory was that there are no significant differences between the genders so we must teach and treat them the same. That lame idea failed, so the post-modern view is to acknowledge some gender differences, but insist on some form of egalitarianism. Put simply, this is still trying to make two inherently unequal beings equal—round pegs in square holes. The alternative is to thank God for the differences between boys and girls and find a way to teach that, generally speaking, meets the basic needs of all children. *Teach* them similarly (using what works), but *treat* them differently.

In the classical, Christian school revival, we believe we have found (by learning from the past) that common means of teaching. We ground our philosophy of education on two foundations: first, the rock-bed is the Bible. In it, God makes no differences in the purposes or content for educating children based on gender. He created both and says they both must learn His moral and natural laws. The second level of our foundation, built upon the first, is an ancient means of instruction. We teach using the classical Trivium (Grammar, Logic, and Rhetoric). This gives us a varied, but sequential plan for instruction that has shown itself effective in generations past, far longer than any modern fling or fad for successful teaching. We further encourage the students to use their God-given differences to *assist* each other, wherever possible, instead of mocking each others' gender-related weaknesses. This includes teaching old-fashioned etiquette: you know, boys holding doors for girls, girls being encouraged to act lady-like, etc., as well as practical, tutorial assistance to each other in and out of the classroom. This contributes to the overall positive tone of the classroom and school, which in turn affects learning.

We fundamentally believe that God really does know best and He makes all children, with all their distinct traits. Then He commands parents to teach them well, without worrying about "equality." Let's study our children, but relax, and let them be who they are, as we train them in ways that are best for all.

How Can School Policies and Guidelines Reinforce the Biblical Model of Family?

You think it would be obvious to anyone in Christian education that a Christian school should actively support the biblical home pattern. But just as there are guys who ride motorcycles without helmets, there are Christian schools by the score who don't get this point. Lip service in a neatly framed mission statement doesn't count for much. But it is where you begin:

Published goals/philosophy of the school clearly illustrate support of the biblical home (and yes, you still accept kids from non-biblical homes because ALL families were created by God).

The school head authorities (board, administration) should have a familial connection to the school, in other words they are parents themselves, as much as possible.

In the hiring/interviewing process for staff—deference should be given to the wishes, directions of the husband, or consideration of the wife's feelings. For single folks, what is their parents' view of taking this job? (Even if non-Christian parents—you're getting the idea, by now, I trust.)

In student disciplinary policies, guidelines—Is Dad the one called and acknowledged as the primary person the student is accountable to? Should be. Do you have ways of recognizing and stepping away from situations where the school has become the best and/or only disciplinarian?

When academic difficulties arise—The school should act as the advising servant, not the professional leader in decision-making. Active parental decisiveness is required, not suggested. From the school's side, parental leadership should be deferred to, not railed against, even in private discussions among the staff.

In conducting extra-curricular activities—Is there built-in consideration and deference given to family priorities? No, not a Burger King approach ("have it your way"), but a well-designed, reasonable program, then leave it up to parents to chose which to participate in. This is a prime area for the school to illustrate its understanding and encouragement of commitments.

Handling non-school programs aimed at children—What is the school's response to legitimate and illegitimate advertisements? DARE, university living groups, parks-and-rec, Kiwanis, local churches, etc. All will want to get something "out" to your kids and families. The school can tacitly undermine the parents' authority by granting access to the kids from objectionable groups or programs. Carefully screen each for any similarity of philosophy to your school's, generally say no to most advertisements. Simply put, whatever goes home should have the support of your school

In many ways the most dangerous and least obvious area for undermining parental authority—student/staff relations. A kid with an empty emotional "tank" (lacking love and attention) will look to get that tank filled. Christian schools are hardly immune from real or perceived improper relations between teachers and students, particularly between teenage girls and male secondary teachers. Here is a recipe for disaster: Take one lonely, low-tanked, young lady whose father has failed her needs. Add one sincere, kind, ready-to-counsel, male high school teacher. Mix in a warm, quiet setting for almost any length of time. Serve up cold with deadly consequences. Empty tanks should not be ignored. Appropriate hugs and kind words should not be withheld from any child. But only the love of parents can fill those tanks.

There are many other areas and ways the school will or won't support the biblical home. Obviously, there will need to be allowances for unique situations—divorces, financial problems, single-parent homes, etc. No policy or guideline is a perfect, one-size fits all in dealing with families. You will frequently need Solomon's wisdom. Keep records, refer to your board for support and leadership in awkward, one-time decisions. Be wary of extending credit in rocky family times—it is not necessarily a favor to them or the school.

The Big "E"—Evangelism

Probably the greatest and most persistent challenge to the primary duties of the home that arises in Christian schools is the issue of "Christian character building," salvation, and just general spiritual training. Where are the lines? You HAVE to answer and clearly address the question of *what is your school's role in the spiritual lives of the kids?*

For example, do you buy the following? It's a popular theme:

"Christian schools have the unique, God-given privilege of providing more than a primary, Bible-based education. The PRIMARY goal of every Christian school should be that each child come to know Jesus Christ as Savior and grow in Him to full Christian maturity. Young lives should be changed for eternity! Yet many Christian schools are not fulfilling their unique mission of bringing God into the center of their students' lives."

The author goes on: *"The home and church should also be working to this end. But since the children are taught in the classroom many more hours per week than at home or church, the Christian school is a primary place for children to strengthen their walk with God. Lenin said, "Give me four years to teach the children, and the seed I have sown will never be uprooted." Imagine the impact your school can have not only for the present generation but for many to come if you use the time you have wisely.*" (To be fair, the author did not work in a Christian school nor does he seem to remember that Lenin was a communist and a God-hater!) Is that your view, too?

Certainly we want children to become believers and grow in grace and truth. But WHO is to take responsibility for this? The author unabashedly says the Christian school. Do you agree? The Bible, i.e. the Holy God, doesn't. He rather clearly leaves such a critical issue with the parents (Deut. 6, Eph. 6, most of Proverbs, etc.). Much as you (and your teachers) will love these kids and want them to walk with God, remember: they are not *yours*! Trust God for them and help the families as much as possible. That's all you can and *should* do.

CHAPTER SIX

Discipline Standards

Once again, your philosophy will come through loud and clear not in what you say about discipline, but what you *do*. I can't emphasize enough the difference between what is written and what is actually done. Everybody looks good on paper, especially if they get to write the paper. To get you started, at least, here is a copy of our current policy:

10.4 Discipline Policy

Dates: Approved September 21, 1992

Revised: February 21, 2000

Objectives: To ensure consistent biblical discipline at Logos School.

Scope: This policy applies to all students enrolled at Logos School.

Definitions: N/A

Guidelines:

1. The kind and amount of discipline (punishment) will be determined by the teachers, and if necessary, the principal and superintendent. The discipline will be administered in the light of the individual student's problem and attitude.

2. The discipline will be based on biblical principles, e.g. restitution, apologies (public and private), swift/painful punishment, restoration of fellowship, no lingering attitudes, etc.
3. The vast majority of discipline problems are to be dealt with at the classroom level.
4. In order to maintain consistency, secondary teachers will regularly meet together to discuss biblical standards and school policy concerning discipline.
5. Love and forgiveness will be an integral part of the discipline of a student.
6. Office Visits: There are five basic behaviors that will automatically necessitate discipline from the principal (versus the teacher). Those behaviors are:
    - Disrespect shown to any staff member. The staff member will be the judge of whether or not disrespect has been shown.
    - Dishonesty in any situation while at school, including lying, cheating, and stealing.
    - Rebellion, i.e. outright disobedience in response to instructions.
    - Fighting, i.e. striking in anger with the intention to harm the other student(s).
    - Obscene, vulgar, or profane language, as well as taking the name of the Lord in vain.
7. During the visit with the principal, the principal will determine the nature of the discipline. The principal may require restitution, janitorial work, parental attendance during the school day with their child, formal attire to be worn by the student to school, spanking, or any other measures consistent with biblical guidelines which may be appropriate.
8. If for any of the above, or other reasons, a student receives

discipline from the principal, the following accounting will be observed within the school year:

- The first two times a student is sent to the principal for discipline the student's parents will be contacted and given the details of the visit. The principal will make a note of each occasion when the parents are contacted after an office visit, and enter that record in the students' file. The parents' assistance and support in averting further problems will be sought.
- The third office visit will be followed by a meeting with the student's parents, principal, and superintendent.
- Should the student require a fourth office visit, a two-day suspension will be imposed on the student.
- If a fifth office visit is required, the student will be expelled from the school.

9. If a student commits an act with such serious consequences that the principal deems it necessary, the office-visit process may be by-passed and suspension or expulsion imposed immediately. Examples of such serious misconduct could include: acts endangering the lives of other students or staff members, gross violence, vandalism of school property, violations of civil law, or any act in clear contradiction to scriptural commands. Students may be subject to school discipline for serious misconduct which occurs after school hours.
10. At the discretion of the appropriate principal, a student may be refused re-enrollment for the following school year. Such refusal to re-enroll is not considered a direct disciplinary act, requiring accumulated office visits in order to be taken. Refusal to re-enroll is not the equivalent of suspension or expulsion.
11. Should an expelled or non-re-enrolled student desire to be readmitted to Logos School at a later date, the Logos School Board, or its delegated committee, will make a decision

> based on the student's attitude and circumstances at the time of re-applying.

So, that's our policy. Probably not that different in appearance from many others. And it doesn't have to be that *different*, as though being unique is a virtue. No, it just has to be enforced, followed, adhered to, done in every situation, with an even hand, great wisdom and diligence, while showing no favoritism. Every time, all the time. Is my point coming through? Well, of course!, you say. Who wouldn't understand that?

The problem is not with the understanding. It's the doing: it *isn't* done.

You see, disciplining students (as in correcting attitudes and actions), isn't supposed to be easy or enjoyable, but it should be satisfying because it produces good fruit, when done well.

Obviously a policy is rarely all that needs to be said about any aspect of the school, especially something as foundational and varied as the discipline of students. Many books have been written on ways to maintain classroom control and management. Some are even good. How to spot them? Well, ideally they should be written by Christians, for starters. But there are secular writers who actually use biblical wisdom, too. They just don't know it. Pick those to read and develop a fuller view of what you want in your school.

Within our school, we have developed a few administrative guidelines and related principles that we expect the teachers to consistently enforce:

"Three strikes and you're out!"—This looks a bit different in each grade (the lower grades use popsicle sticks in cans), but the basic idea is the same. If a child acts up to the point of needing to be personally, verbally corrected, his name goes on the board (or his stick moves to the next can). If, in the same day, he requires another correction, a check goes by his name and he loses recess time. A third time, as you might guess from the title, means he takes a trip to the principal's office. There, depending on the Solomon-like wisdom of the principal, the child may or may not get a spanking (yes, we still do that out in pre-historic Idaho).

Now the child has had his first "office visit" and may be on the road to five visits and expulsion. Thankfully, the vast majority of students rarely get to a third visit. By adhering to this simple, little enforcement of three strikes, our teachers don't have to reach red-faced exasperation before they remove the hooligan.

Parental notification—No matter what punishment is meted out in the office, the principal contacts the parents, particularly the dad, as soon afterwards as appropriate. Typically that means a phone call that evening to explain what happened and answer any questions. The wise principal encourages the now wiser child to tell his parents first, *before* he, the principal, calls the home. It is critical to remember that the principal is reporting in to the *real* authorities to tell them what he did in their name.

"**Moving the line**"—It happens that we have Johnny-wise-guy once in a while who knows how to play the system. He can get two counts each day and not cross over the line to get the third, and all that that entails. If the teacher observes this pattern (a pattern is any event happening three or more times), then she can, with the principal's and parents' concurrence, move the line back to TWO counts and he's "outa there!"

Basic etiquette—This may seem like an odd topic to throw in here, but I believe it has a lot to do with the overall tone and behavior in the classroom, as well as the whole school. Simply put, we have found that requiring good old-fashioned, but biblically justifiable, manners is a good way to get what you want in the class, while encouraging love in the details. For instance, we require the boys to lead by serving—they hold doors for the girls, wait for the girls to go first in line, and stand by the lunch tables until the girls are seated first. We require all of the students to stand when an adult enters the room, as well as usually standing to answer a question from the teacher. Give it a try: you might like what you see as a result.

BOY MEETS GIRL

They were obviously a bit impatient, shuffling and yet tense, eager to depart the classroom in one explosive rush. But the teacher insisted they wait, even if it was a bit longer than usual. The last few girls were still gathering their personal items and heading out the door. Then, as the last young lady passed into the hallway, the teacher reminded the boys to "walk, not run" on their way to the lunchroom. They obeyed, but their steps were jerky, like a Ferrari having to drive 25 mph on an open stretch of highway. A good and necessary practice of self-control, with some outside encouragement, of course.

As most of our Logos parents know by now, for several years we have been highlighting the need for upgrading the cultural aspects of our school. One significant form this has taken is in the area of etiquette. Put in biblical language, this is practicing love in the details. "Details" in this case means the small opportunities we have every day to show consideration for others. Even more specifically, we are encouraging the children to make distinctions in how they show consideration for the opposite gender. The Bible is clear about these distinctions so we believe we should be also, regardless of our culture's never-say-die crusade to eliminate them.

So, for instance, in every grade, the boys are required to allow the girls to leave the classroom first. In the lunchroom, as they file in, the boys are to stand until the girls are seated. Young men are to hold doors for young women and ladies. (This has had the side-effect of young men frequently holding doors even for older, er, mature male teachers and principals.) During secondary assemblies, the young men are to watch for ladies standing in the back and assist in getting a chair for them. What are the girls and young ladies supposed to do for their part? How do they show consideration for their male peers? By treating the boys' deference to them with respect, not scorn or mockery. A thankful attitude is pretty much all that's required.

Are we just trying to hark back to the lost age of chivalry in some pathetic, anachronistic manner? After all,our mascot is a knight. Aren't we kicking against the current social goads, or even worse, not preparing the kids for the "real world" out there, where the sexes are really the same?

No, to all the above. For one thing, the age of chivalry was hardly one we'd like to emulate—it was largely adulterous and generally without a biblical foundation. As for the "real world," by whose definition? God made us male and female and until He rewires us, that's what we are.

Our goal in this, as with every other aspect of the education we provide, is to seek to prepare the students to think biblically about all they will face before and after graduation. That includes the rather critical, life-changing aspect of being married. To be clear: we are not going into the realm of marital counseling, child-rearing, or even providing home management courses, per se.

But we certainly recognize that a young man doesn't turn into a gentleman, knowing how to show consideration for a young lady, by merely turning eighteen, or twenty-one, for that matter. He becomes what he has been practicing to be since he was old enough to observe the model of older men. If he has never seen a gentleman in action or been required to act like one at five, twelve and fifteen years old, he simply won't burst into one later, at the point when it matters to him. That is, when he meets a young lady to whom he does want to show special consideration. The ugly caterpillar won't become the impressive butterfly just by wishing.

To up the ante, God designed most people for the state of marriage. As Paul tells us, He grants a few folks a special gift of singleness. This means that the vast majority of those sweet little faces coming to kindergarten each morning are heading for either a God-honoring marriage or possibly a series of heart-rending, self-centered relationships. That sounds kind of harsh put that way, but the facts and figures of the "real world" bear this out.

The only question that we face as a Christian school then is, in regard to those facts of life, what kind of behavior will we model and enforce for our students? Will we tacitly adopt the world's view and pretend that how boys and girls treat each other at school is of no consequence to marriage later on? Or will we, under the limited, delegated authority of our parents, seek to model and require the kind of countless, small considerations husbands should demonstrate to their wives and wives to their husbands? Which approach is really denying the reality to come in the lives of these students? Which approach encourages the biblical mandate that young men are to treat young women "as sisters, in all purity and respect?"

There is a lot to how boys and girls are to interact, wherever they are or how old they are. Suffice it to say here, in all matters of the mind and heart of a student, the Scripture and its principles are neither inappropriate or outdated.

Undergirding principles—In all our discipline, there are key biblical principles that should be present and followed. They include:

- Listening to all sides before making a judgment. Justice doesn't rush or have a bias toward one party over the other. It's amazing how many times "good" kids are the actual culprits, not just the chronic offender.
- Never discipline in anger or frustration.
- If punishment is necessary, it should follow the judgment in a prompt manner. Students shouldn't be made to wonder when the ax is going to fall, so to speak.
- Punishment should be painful. Even though your school may not have the liberty (due to restrictive, unbiblical state laws) to spank the child, somebody at home should. As the children grow older, the spanks should diminish and other costly punishments should take their place, more in keeping with making physical restitution. But restitution should always be addressed where necessary, e.g. asking forgiveness from the teacher and/or others.
- Just as the sin should be clearly identified, so should the love and forgiveness be clearly expressed once the child has confessed and sought forgiveness. "Apologizing" is not the same thing as seeking forgiveness. I can't mention it too much; you have to get, read, keep and apply the principles in Jay Adam's book, *From Forgiven to Forgiving.* Best thing on the market for Christians dealing with Christians.
- Just as we are restored to a right relationship to the Father in Christ whenever we sin, a restored relationship should be sought and realized after any discipline situation. This should be the norm, not just sometimes. There will be the occasional unrepentant child. If necessary, have his parents come and get him. Don't belabor it and try to be

the Holy Spirit, or even his folks. Let them deal with him at home.

School cultural considerations

Repairing the ruins of education includes a view to recapturing the cultural areas, and even terminology that we've surrendered to the pagans (believe me, this is something we will be working on for years to come). But it's very necessary to pursue in our schools.

What is the historical understanding of worthwhile components of real culture, and education? Truth, beauty, and goodness: A very necessary, parallel trivium to the classical model. Otherwise we're putting new wine into old wineskins; look beyond the core of what we do, i.e. strong academics, cutting with the grain by teaching to student characteristics, reinstating the preeminence of quality literature. Our core needs a nourishing outer cover, all that surrounds and supports the curricular trivium. We are just now finding the peach pit—let's not ignore the surrounding tasty flesh of the peach—even if it is a little fuzzy!

We must provide a full-orbed view of what we are trying to recover, from top to bottom, inside out.

How do we define Truth, Beauty, and Goodness? Particularly a Christian, medieval understanding of expressions of God's character to us. Thomas Aquinas refers to Truth, Beauty and Goodness as "transcendentals," i.e. divine aspects that are ever present and apparent to us because they reflect God. No one aspect can be understood apart from the others.

Truth—The unalterable absolutes particularly about and from God—e.g. Jesus Christ is God Incarnate.

Goodness—The unalterable absolutes about morality, purity, relations to each other and God, e.g. Love thy neighbor, as thy self.

Beauty—The unalterable absolutes that reflect the divine creation in its goodness, and that as it reflects the beauty of holiness (truth and goodness), e.g. order, peace, symmetry, harmony, light, color, etc.

Defining culture within our schools should not be reactionary (a list of all we DON'T WANT), lest we become legalistic. That's just saying "no" to the more advanced symptoms of the disease, but never asking what the illness is or why we're sick. We need to be culturally informed but seeking a new, or better yet, a *revived* center of what is "normal"—why should we act as though it's the world's backyard and they have the only football? So we say we won't play their game, but we sit on the sidelines and watch somewhat longingly? Or at least our kids do.

We need to take another look at the arts and their benefits, not just instruction—not make the gnostics' mistake of believing ourselves and teaching our kids that material is bad, spiritual is good! Compelled to examine all things and hold to that which is good—and true and beautiful (Phil. 4:8)!

So, in our schools then, what the academic disciplines are to the mind, and scriptural application should be to the heart, the exposure to the arts should be to the soul—making it full of pleasant richness for students. After all, school forms the cultural epicenter of their lives, especially as they look beyond their family for what is culturally "the norm." School and all its symbols, aesthetics, and messages fill their lives. Our students should be full people in every sense—along with their parents. We want to try to give them fat souls!

Where we should focus (for starters) in applying Beauty

Sample themes—visual art, music: vocal, instrumental, dance, drama, poetry, etiquette—don't automatically start thinking along standard lines, e.g. how do we make time for these as programs? Relax, let these names be more like warm, mouth-watering smells drifting out from behind the kitchen door, tantalizing and peaking your hunger, rather than regarding them like so many frozen vegetables you throw in to just add green to a meal.

We're not advocating a school for the arts, i.e. hours of technical training, rather arts for a school climate, which many of our Christian school brothers either notoriously ignore or, at best, give a 1950s nod to the arts, e.g. Noah's Ark coloring books. You might have noticed that our dark-minded, sentimental, liberal counterparts are starting private schools (now being federally blessed as charter schools for fundings' sake) that advertise rhythmic movement and exploratory Native American tattooing, while listening to Appalachian zither music. There must be a better application, one that enhances, not detracts from or replaces a solid education.

Make no mistake, since Ugly is the new norm/expectation, only a planned counter-attack, not a defensive posture, will win the day. In our post-modern era all ideas are tolerable as long as they are do not seek to replace others by ascendancy, i.e. just saying no to their ways does not incite any reaction and is just plain limp. Re-claiming territory already surrendered *will* get a reaction (even among believers), but it is what we're commanded to do.

Lest we think modem Ameri-Christendom knows how to define beauty or culture—consider the majority of Christian musicians, gift store kitsch, Thomas Kinkade/Precious Moments "art" vs. Giotto, Rembrandt, and Bach. If our Christian gift-stores reflect the best arsenal we have to win back lost territory, we better assume the position of the Iraqi soldiers in the last days of the Gulf War—hands way up and surrender even to photographers! Instead, look at and study what we had and why, when Christendom drove the arts!

Planning and accomplishing the new center—follow the Trivium

Grammar level—We want to fill their school lives with beauty, make it part of their landscape and vocabulary; training in *visual arts*—basic painting/drawing/sculpting techniques, great works and names, integration with as many disciplines as possible, e.g. drawing in science and history; *great music*—sing and hear, play CDs for classroom music; room decor not just primary colors and make-it, take-it materials; *drama*—act out great tales, planned assemblies, assign parts in Shakespeare readings, get them comfortable in front of room and on stage; *dance*—PE "exercises," historic dances to historic music (yes, boys and girls together); *poetry*—literature, but integrate with history, appreciate various types, children's and adult poets; *etiquette*—boys as gentlemen, girls as ladies, make as well as look for opportunities to practice deference and respect.

Logic level—Now they need to learn, practice, experience structures undergirding earlier "vocabulary" of culture; formal classes in art, music, drama productions (all of the highest possible caliber, not kitsch), opportunities to present skills to rest of school/public at functions;

speech meets, debates enhancing personal presence and presentation, as well as knowledge; continue dance (waltzes, polkas, etc.) in PE; dress and etiquette requirements notch up.

Rhetoric level—Now we can expect to see and hear inculcated values and knowledge of what is truly worthwhile and beautiful; we give them formal opportunities to express their understandings; classes in arts continue with higher expectations (Masters works); high school drama performances that elicit unabashed praises, not sympathetic noises (Why not *Much Ado, vs. Nightmare High School?);* speeches, theses presentations and defenses; formal balls, swing dancing—unleashing the joy and rigor of dance with polished self-control; Protocol training and events; opportunities to train younger students—mini-conferences in school, graduation—the hallmark of solemn joyfulness, or "solempne."

If we build it, they will notice and wonder

Phil. 2—As a manifestation of the light they have, our students' joy in their historic, yay verily, medieval culture will shine out in a dark, joyless culture: Why are those Christians having so much fun? vs. the lament of one of the early Christian rock stars—"Why does the devil have all the good music?"

Our kids learn that life in Christ is indeed life, abundantly rich and beautiful! They won't want less, but more, for their own children.—The restoration of culture, no King but King Jesus!

In all this discussion on discipline, that old reprobate, Ben Franklin, had some wisdom we might apply: "An ounce of prevention is worth a pound of cure." Discipline is not just punishment, it's training. If we do our jobs well and give the teachers what they need to do theirs well, most of the kids we have in the school will find great joy and peace in obeying. That, too, is good discipline.

CHAPTER SEVEN

Curriculum planning

And the Winner Is ... Pedagogy or Particulars?

ACCS is now just over ten years old. There are about 140 schools with their own distinctive looks and culture, which is natural and appropriate. *All* of us, regardless of the age of our school, are just at the beginning of recovering classical schooling. Therefore, it's not at all surprising that we haven't gotten past the first and foremost question: What is the essence of a classical education and how should it *look*? For the sake of this writing I am assuming that you are familiar with what has become common terminology in the revival of classical education: the trivium (grammar, logic, rhetoric), the corresponding three stages Sayers lays out for children's growth: poll-parrot, pert and poetic, the emphasis on Latin as historically and linguistically necessary, worldview thinking, all subjected to the infallible Word of God. I am not going to go over those basics here.

But at the heart of what we call the classical school movement or revival are living, breathing teachers who may understand the above terminology, but who may have little if any idea of how that is to affect their actual *teaching*! If your classical school does what many do, in your first or even subsequent years of teaching, you were handed a pack of curriculum materials, some even in solid, heavy books, and were told to go forth and teach classically. Maybe you were even given some brief instruction in Gregory's *Seven Laws*. But then what *actually* happened in your classroom instruction? Assuming you had some knowledge of or prior experience with typical teaching methods, did your being in that classical school make a significant difference in the *way* you taught? Or was the difference from any previous teaching experience largely in how much and *what* you taught? What occupied your attention more, the *way* or the *what*? My premise here is that only one of those can take precedence. And the difference in each is stark and critical to your teaching and your school's success.

I have had the privilege to visit a good number of sister schools around the country, sometimes to do training, others more formally as an ACCS accreditation team member. Many of these schools have similar rigorous curriculum course work, academic requirements and even behavioral standards. In the documentation packages I receive ahead of time, the school's work can look very impressive, on paper. But one serious downfall that the subsequently un-accredited schools also share is that all those great ideals and curriculum materials didn't make a difference in the *way* the teachers taught in the classroom! And it was that disconnection that most often made the difference in the school not receiving accreditation.

Not a race, but a wrestling match

So what is to be the necessary difference in instruction and consideration of content? Perhaps an analogy may help to illustrate the conflict.

As in most wrestling, except so-called professional wrestling, there are usually just two combatants vying to be on top. In our educational game, these combatants are **pedagogy** and **particulars** or content:

Pedagogy: That is, the skills and rules of teaching. This necessitates a well-thought out approach to teaching, its dynamics, skills, influence, well summed up in Gregory's *Seven Laws*. This emphasis requires a thorough understanding of the students' frames and how they understand and apply the lesson.

Particulars: That is, the content choices, emphases of the written program. This is what we call the curriculum or course work a school sets out for its students. The classical movement has certainly produced a welcome revival of interest in teaching great and lasting literature, ancient languages, primary documents and a stress on what used to be the content of a rigorous education. A worthwhile but, albeit, tall order.

The nature of the competition—one's got to be top dog

Both of these competitors, the skill of teaching and the curriculum content, obviously must be considered in our schools. Both will and should have a very powerful impact on the students. But both cannot be given equal emphasis—one *will* shape, guide and have priority over the other. Why do I say that? Because both of these necessary components in our schools are strong enough to *single-handedly* shape, guide and lead the entire school's program and greatly affect its quality. Also, both have loyal adherents that stress each one's importance, based on their philosophical leanings. Have you ever had two bosses? Not a pleasant situation. Even if they initially agree on most things, it won't be long before there are employees loyal to one over and against the other boss. Our Lord said a man can only serve one master at a time. Which will it be?

So, back to our wrestling metaphor:

First scenario or match: The content wins, it comes out on top. The hallmark of the school's work then becomes how much and what kind of content the students are exposed to. Sounds reasonable, even desirable. Subsequently the primary determiners of the school's success are high student GPAs and grades, typically heavy homework amounts, standardized tests scores in the nineties, National Merit awards, and other measures of academic prowess. College prep course work takes precedence in time, funding and planning over the actual methods of teaching. How do I know that? Consider: If a teacher does a *extremely* poor job teaching it doesn't matter if the content is high octane: the students will do poorly. No argument. But in a content-driven program, *especially* a classical one, even a *mediocre* teacher can appear successful by trusting in the quality of the material to silence concerns from the less-informed. Also frequently in our schools, the mediocre teacher puts the onus on the many motivated students to work harder to grasp the difficult material.

The teacher can be a johnny-one-note, lecture-fits-all type of instructor and still appear to be successful because the students are bright enough to find a way, scraping and clawing, to spit back Herodotus one-liners on a test. Or worse, they have the necessary acumen to parrot, even at the rhetoric level, the teacher's lofty-sounding opinions. So THAT'S a classical education? Never mind that these same students, like all students who sit under the cram-it-in model, forget at least 50% of what they were taught, almost by the time they cross the stage after getting their diploma! At least their transcripts look impressive....

Second match: Pedagogy wins and so the emphasis of the school is now on *how* the students are taught, and the content takes second place in priority. Now what happens? First off, the teachers are held more accountable. A scary thought for those of us who love the material but not the work it takes to pass it on. In many cases, if they've taught before, teachers have to UN-learn some habits, as well as learn new ones. Mediocrity is quickly evident in teaching because the administration has a high priority on actually working with and evaluating the instruction, with the goal toward real, recognizable and measurable improvement. The students subsequently benefit because the teacher is compelled to teach with the grain, that is, knowing and using the nature and frame of the students. That doesn't necessarily mean seeking to appeal to their desires or all their current interests, but rather studying and using the way they were made. We'll examine this more in a moment.

So, which is easier? Content-driven or teaching priority?

A related question is which is flashier? Human nature will be drawn naturally to the easiest and the flashiest means to get the job done. That's just the way we are. Strange as it may sound, even given the cost and complexity of high power content materials, I will maintain that content-driven programs are easier than making pedagogy the priority. It just takes money and you can buy the best "stuff." In fact, that stuff is getting easier to find since so many of us are using it. Given time, just like the government school text book publishers, we will likely see teacher editions, helps, keys, maps, and clever workbooks for the *Iliad*. Maybe they're already out there. That may not be all bad; the *Iliad is* a wonderful story. But remember: human nature thrives on seeking the easier path. It is also very heady to tout the hefty classes and materials our students use. Anyone who knows anything about education knows that Homer trumps Home Ec. when it comes to sounding academic. When the vast majority of students in government high school are studying famous lesbian artists in American Cultural Studies, while *our* kids are reading the *Code of Hammurabi* in the original languages and developing cold fusion as homework, it can be tempting to be puffed up a bit.

Another reason I say it's easier to rely on content instead of quality instruction is that it's easier on the teacher. Yes, it's a lot of work to read and prep to teach the content we likely never learned. But that can mean just filling our own heads with more "stuff." Of itself, it doesn't require us to change our day-to-day teaching practices. It appears that an eighth law of teaching might exist. It's this: Unless a teacher is thoroughly compelled and taught to teach otherwise, he will teach as he was taught. We can't help it. Most of us were taught the same way in our formative years—that is, teachers essentially telling us stuff and then testing us to see if we found a way to remember it, at least until the test time. That's it. So, it's like a law of physics—we will teach in one teaching direction, i.e. the way *our* teachers taught, unless some forceful object gets in our path and brings us to an abrupt halt and/or turns us in a new direction.

Re-tooling our *teaching*, instead of relying on great content.

First, look at the students, then cut with the grain....

Teaching classically, i.e. with a view toward preparing them for future learning, requires that we re-examine the way we view the students and their growth. Dorothy Sayers noted three levels, poll-parrot, pert, and poetic. She was adopting the premise of beginning formal education at about eight years old (based on the historical, Greco-Roman model). But we have five through seven year-olds. They are profoundly different than their third grade fellow students and require specific, well thought-out preparation for the "full" grammar stage. So, we must teach to four, not just three, levels and their corresponding characteristics.

The students in this *pre-polly* stage, as we have named it (keeping with the alliteration), are very sensory driven and, like the older grammar students, are not deep thinkers. But they are quite a bit younger and, at this point, that means a great deal. They still need us to help them make some sense out of the world and more particularly, the way to learn about it. (See the *Tools Chart*.) This is a crucial time in which we can help them build mental "shelves" upon which later material will be "stacked," mostly through memorization. We do this by using all the students' senses to our advantage. They are still young enough to enjoy tasting, touching, moving, singing, hearing as ways of gaining more understanding. Their senses are like five-lane highways all flowing into their brains and at their age traffic is flowing well in all lanes. Why not use those lanes? It won't be too long before these students get older and, as with most adults, the lanes narrow to about two, sight and hearing, for most brain-traffic. Consider: Why do our grandmothers remember the little songs and poems from their youth? It's probably *not* because of the intrinsic value of the content, but rather because of HOW they learned them. That is, most likely through repetition, singing, chanting, at a particularly appropriate time when those techniques appealed so much.

Then the poll-parrot, pert, and poetic students need us to use the same approach. That is consider their natural, God-given strengths and affinities, then arrange and tailor our chosen content to fit the classical teaching methods we employ.

Remember where we got the trivium, from the first three of the seven liberal arts. It was a *way* of learning how to learn so that when the students mastered the learning techniques in grammar, logic or dialectic and rhetoric, they could move into the hard core academic content of the quadrivium: geometry, music, arithmetic and astronomy.

Preparing, Not Packing

Lest it be lost in other points, let me state unequivocally: I love the great content of most classical curriculums. It is like discovering a long abandoned cache of fine, well-aged wine. It is because I hate to see its value diminished through poor use that I write this. Old wine, as our Lord pointed out, shouldn't go into new wineskins. The "new wineskins" we too often grab are the poor teaching methods of the last couple of generations.

How then does this mis-match and wrong prioritization of content over pedagogy show up?

Pacing or racing?

The temptation to race to the fire can easily outweigh the value of thoughtful pacing. In spite of hearing wise counsel to the contrary, there are many new classical educators who are striving in one generation to regain what was lost over centuries. "Why can't all these kids be Cotton Mathers? At least by next year!" To hear some folks, they won't be pleased until their second graders have memorized the Pentateuch in Hebrew or their first graders are working trigonometry. This is a disservice not only to the students, but to the value to be gained in studying that material with the appropriate maturity and background. Understanding and teaching to the students' frames requires that we push, challenge and support, but not make the content odious or tedious by cramming too much in too fast.

So much to teach, so little recollection

There is a tremendous amount of wonderful material and knowledge out there! If content were everything, the be-all and end-all of education, then personally I would advocate for a whole year of history spent on Theodore Roosevelt. It could easily be done. But Scripture calls us to strive and yearn for wisdom, not the mere accumulation of facts or even knowledge. A wise man may not recall everything he was taught. But he will know *how* to gain or re-gain knowledge, if he was taught well. Students will and do forget tons of what we spent so many intensive hours feeding them. Frankly, if remembrance of material is the only point, we of all people are most to be pitied!

Forgetting their frame for the fame of our name.

That's a little ditty to take to heart as a warning (forged in a grammatical style) that sums up my points above. As educators in the classical revival, we *are* making strides in providing a better education for our children than the one we had. That can be easily documented. But we mustn't think it's because of the impressive content we use. We can so easily be puffed up and take ungodly pride in our school, our movement because of the "stuff." The kids will see through that facade, and the saddest part is that though *we* certainly value our content, if we are just stuffing it in them, they will come to regard our gems of knowledge as just so much "stuff."

The balance of pedagogical priorities and content can be a wrestling match, but it should not be a war. They are not enemies, seeking to destroy each other. But they are inherently competitive. We should obviously seek to apply the strengths of both because both are *necessary* priorities to our students' education. And they are best kept in balance by knowing that teaching should lead and the content should follow. Perhaps another analogy might be appropriate here. Imagine you have two good friends who you would like to introduce to each other. Since you care deeply for both of them you are rather sure they will be pleased to meet each other. Your introduction is critical and will get their friendship off on the right foot. Now imagine that one of your friends is a student and the other "friend" is the marvelous material you want to introduce to your student. Your "introduction" is critical. It will also take quite some time. Shouldn't you give it a good bit of thought so these two friends might want to get to know each other better?

Paul told Timothy "But the goal of our instruction is love from a pure heart and a good conscience and a sincere faith. For some men, straying from these things, have turned aside to fruitless discussion" (I Tim 1:5,6). If biblical instruction is our model and it seeks to change minds and hearts, not just impart knowledge, shouldn't our instruction of admittedly less value seek to inspire, challenge and prepare our students? If we focus only on cramming them full of knowledge, even worthwhile knowledge, I fear we are ignoring the scriptural admonishment to "not boil a kid in its mother's milk" (Ex. 23:19). We will use what should be gently and thoughtfully fed to them and cause them to hate what should be precious. Productive, classical instruction enables the students to digest the great feast of knowledge. Then not only will they love to *keep* learning, they will love *what* they learned!

"We have lost the tools of learning ... that were so adaptable to all tasks. What use is it to pile task upon task and prolong days of labor, if at the close

the chief object is left unattained? For the sole end of education is this: ***to teach men how to learn for themselves*** *and whatever instruction fails to do this is effort spent in vain." -Dorothy Sayers*

"Give instruction to a wise man, and he will be still wiser; teach a righteous man, and he will increase his learning." *-Proverbs 9:9*

A FEW THOUGHTS ON HOMEWORK

This will be brief even though the topic of homework can afflict schools with all the vigor and fun of an outbreak of head lice. Parents, in other words, can get a tad bit over-heated when it appears to them that the teachers are a) Assigning too much homework, and/or b) Assigning unclear or too difficult homework. If you DON'T hear some concerns in your early years especially about homework, you will be the amazing exception. So, some thoughts:

Since homework, at any level, takes time at home, it should not be assigned due to the teacher's poor planning of class time, or in place of an assignment that could have been completed at school. Your teachers and their plans should reflect a good amount of reality.

Homework (or any school work, for that matter) should not be used as a means of punishment for poor behavior. What are we saying when we treat assignments like a spanking?

The necessity for doing homework will vary somewhat from grade to grade, as well as from one academic discipline to another. How homework is approached by the student will also vary according to the propensities of the student. Frequently you will have perfectionistic young ladies who treat each assignment as though it were to be enshrined in the National Archives. They turn an hour's assignment into a ten hour ordeal. Then you might have young men who write their semester's thesis paper on the day it is due, on the way to school, in pencil ... on the back of their lunch bag. They turn an hour's assignment into a disaster. Then somewhere in between those extremes, you find kids who tell their parents they spend three hours each evening closeted in their room "working" on homework. When in reality, the three hours breaks down to something like this:

- 45 minutes—Munching Pringle's chips, staring into space
- 45 minutes—Bobbing their head to the music and wandering around the room with headphones 20 minutes—Coming downstairs for snack and pop refills
- 15 minutes—Going to the bathroom, combing their hair, etc.
- 25 minutes—Calling a friend to "ask questions about the assignment" 30 minutes—Actual work on homework
- TOTAL TIME USED = 180 minutes or three hours! Whew.

Certainly you will have a goodly portion of students who actually use their time well. Just a tip: If you are ever curious how much time is being spent on homework by any students, do a survey of a whole class or grade of families. The results should be enlightening and, if the teachers are doing their jobs well, the results should encourage you. They can then be used to reassure concerned parents that the problem may not be the school's. Hint, hint.

There are some practical ways to ensure that your teachers are indeed assigning reasonable amounts and kinds of homework. Here are a few ideas:

At the elementary level, give each grade an average per night. For instance, even first graders could do about twenty minutes of math or spelling work frequently at home. By sixth grade, an hour should be the maximum, and maybe not every night.

At the secondary level, it takes more coordination among the staff. You will have to make sure this happens.

Establish major assignment days for each discipline (history gets Friday, math gets Tuesday, etc.). This avoids the Friday=dump-day for the students.

Make weekly calendars of major assignment (tests, papers) that the teachers fill in and then send home to parents. This helps the teachers also to see what others are requiring of "their" kids.

Prioritize certain disciplines above others with the privilege of giving homework on a regular basis. For instance, math, Latin and English should get the lion's share due to the need for regular practice outside of class time. On the other hand, Bible, history and science shouldn't need much outside time, except to study for a test or complete a project.

There should be an overall average amount of homework time (two hours or so) that is communicated to the parents and the teachers as being reasonable and enforced.

Parents should be reminded that you respect the fact that they know their children's abilities better than you or the teachers do. Therefore, if their child is regularly doing more than the average amount or the work is frequently overwhelming, the parents should feel free to tell their child to stop and go to bed. Then they should inform the teachers of the problem.

As I said above, this is just a brief overview of what I know can be a touchy and significant problem in our schools. The longer you work with, review, revise and communicate your program, the fewer problems you should have in this area, if that's some comfort.

What do we mean by a "Curriculum Guide?" Distinguo!

"Curriculum," the word itself, comes from the Latin 'currere' which referred to a "course" or circuit, as in a race course for horses, runners, or maybe even those great chariot races you see in *Ben Hur*. You can see how this came to be adapted to school work, as so much of athletic and game vocabulary naturally do. To complete a race, the athlete had to complete a given course, especially in a cross-country marathon. The same is true of students through time—to finish their instruction, they had to complete a different kind of course, or curriculum. Unfortunately, most often in our contexts, particularly in Christian education it seems, we are asked what "kind of curriculum" we use. What folks usually mean by that is the specific materials or publisher we use. We mustn't make the same mistake of thinking the materials are synonymous with our chosen curriculum.

More accurately understood, our curriculum choices usually encompass the following:

- All the required (not voluntary, i.e. extra-curricular) work/courses administered and taught within a given **time frame** or period of schooling.

- All the studies and work that the school considers important for its **academic** program.

Then when we add the qualifier, "Guide," as in "to point the way" or "to lead along a path," we get an idea of what a **curriculum guide** should do:

- Determines the **steps** and **pacing**, or sequencing which the curriculum must follow.
- Provides a logical structure for **illustrating** the curriculum requirements.

Where we got ours (a brief testimony):

It amazes me how many schools, even CC ones, don't have a curriculum guide that they've constructed, or even adopted. Most Christian schools simply rely on the "scope and sequence" provided within the purchased publisher's materials. When Logos opened in 1981, the board had already adopted and discussed the Dorothy Sayers's article, *The Lost Tools of Learning,* with our staff. So, though not totally clear on how that philosophy was to look, we purchased a popular Christian publisher's stuff and plunged into the year. It wasn't long (actually about one semester) before we all came to the conclusion that this stuff wasn't doing the job we had envisioned, based on our philosophy. Over the next couple of years, therefore, I met with my small group of teachers and we put together our first curriculum guide. We met over many evenings in our apartment and shared great ideas and deep thoughts like, "What do you think we should expect from kids in third grade math?" But we whacked our first guide out and have continued to modify that guide over the decades. It was very worth doing! Now CC schools have a variety of options in curriculum guides to choose from. You don't have to re-make the proverbial wheel. Nevertheless, whatever you choose, examine it carefully with your staff to see if it is indeed where you want to start.

Some suggested components to include in the guide:

1. A concise philosophy statement for each discipline
2. A breakdown of each separate subject within each grade that includes:
    - Basic materials for teacher and student to use (not every little thing, important ones)
    - List of primary academic objectives (for teacher to address and students to complete)
    - Course description (secondary)
    - Pacing for completing objectives (as appropriate by grade), i.e. how much time should be spent on this material over the course of the year
    - Identified grammar elements: past, present, and those to be reviewed in future (elementary)
3. Basic teaching methodology (classical techniques to be used), list examples you want used!
4. Approximate time taught per week (ranking of importance)
5. Integration suggestions/requirements, i.e. what other material should it reinforce or refer to similar material elsewhere in the curriculum

It doesn't take a software designer to figure out that if you have such a guide to give your teachers that you have just made their lives a whole lot easier. Well, that is your job, isn't it? From the guide your teachers should be able to put together their daily, weekly, quarterly, and semester lesson plans with relative ease. But let's spell it out even more precisely.

Your guide should be built with the following purposes in mind...

1. *Appropriate for children, yet it has lasting value*—Since we are specifically speaking here of the grammar stage, we must give consideration now for the frames of our pupils. Again, the current culture robs children of childhood's richness. Just as C.S. Lewis describes how Susan raced ahead to the

silliest time of life and stayed there, so have generations of us, even perhaps our grandparents as far back as the Roaring 20s, but certainly amplified with the boomers. Look around, there is wonderful food to be had, not only cotton candy. Authors and materials that have shown their value through time. Use these to measure against more recent offerings—there is some good out there. Key here—don't pay too much attention to what's hip in cultural ed; go with what's good.

2. *Challenging, stimulating to mind, heart*—Look back, read again about the strictness, yes, and attention to detail that past generations of youngsters were compelled to exercise. But also look at what they were given as a heritage—and how much they cherished it, when it was done in godliness. All this assumes you are studying children themselves—it would be foolish and a bit presumptuous to ignore the vast gulf between, for instance, the Puritan era and ours. Suffice it to say we have lost more ground than we can know or recover over one generation or even several. But children love to rise to a challenge, when presented well.

3. *Classical—linked to children's growth/characteristics*—Even before Dorothy Sayers, a British mystery writer, and brilliant scholar, the practical teaching aspects that contribute and dovetail so appropriately with the classical trivium were coined by a gentleman, John Milton Gregory, preceding Sayers by about sixty years. His Seven Laws of Teaching include this gem: **"The very language with which new knowledge must be expressed takes its meanings from what is already known and familiar."** From the Law of the Lesson. As with Sayers later, Gregory, a great teacher in his own rite, discovered that tying teaching techniques to the obvious natural characteristics of students just made sense. The Trivium relies on the changing strengths of students.

4. *Integration through natural, obvious lines*—If you've done all that's been presented so far, this will be relatively easy, but

don't rely on most materials to do it for you. If you have gone shopping first, it will be very difficult since most publishers, even Christians, don't plan for this: math is math and history is history. Okay, maybe in a Christian text there will be an attempt to integrate some Bible verse or other into science, but that's about it. Again, no short-cuts! YOU get to do it together as a staff. Examine, consider, plan ways to naturally have material/content reinforce and repeat in various ways.

5. *Constructed from the simple to the complex, known to unknown by logical steps*—So our curriculum and its teaching is integrated not only between the content presented but also by the means of presentation. All disciplines therefore move from the simple to the complex, in somewhat uniform steps, across the years. The third grade teacher knows what came before her and what she is preparing the students to learn in the future. This obviously includes being as sequential as possible, wherever appropriate, e.g. math, spelling, grammar, etc., with material than builds naturally.

6. *Repetitive, cyclical*—John Saxon made his millions (billions?) off the simple concept of repetition, a teaching technique that was understood by the first story tellers and authors of fairy tales, but abandoned by the modern era. Not only is this an effective teaching tool, it needs to be included in our overall curriculum planning by including cycles, instruction that comes around, in greater depth, again and again.

7. *Do more with less (less work for teachers), i.e. limit your disciplines*—It's tempting, I understand, to want to recover all that we've lost in education over generations by tomorrow! Or at least plan for it next year. There is the tendency among our schools to pack it all in rather tightly (10 pounds of stuff in a 5 pound bag, sort of thing). C.S. Lewis made the comment that (at that time) schools taught many subjects lightly, but few things were taught well. It takes time and breadth to truly appreciate just about any thing of worth. Limit what you select

as much as possible, to those disciplines that have natural touch-points with other areas of your curriculum. Obvious things to avoid are any federal or state mandated programs, but even consider how much time everything gets and feel free to limit some for the greater time for others.

What other purposes does a well-designed guide serve?

A well-constructed and frequently upgraded curriculum guide does a number of things for you and more importantly, your staff and parents:

1. *It identifies the school's philosophy and practices*—Everything taught in your school, and I mean everything, MUST have a clear connection and purpose in your classical, Christian philosophy of education. Otherwise, what is being said about that instruction? That you have material that you want to teach to the students, but not take the time to see if it fits your philosophy? Oops.
2. *It distinguishes the school's philosophy and practices*—That is, it distinguishes your school from the thousands of "generic" Christian schools out there. The hallmarks of differences should show up in the curriculum guide. Frankly, that you have a curriculum guide at all will distinguish you, but that's not enough, obviously. The unique elements of your program should be clearly worthwhile and anyone reading your guide should be able to see that fact.
3. *It equips your teachers with a "roadmap" of their year's objectives*—I alluded to this above.
    - It gives the teachers specific "how-to's" for what, when, and why—materials, objectives
    - Gives them necessary information about grades before and after their's (You DO want continuity, don't you?!)
    - If they are new, the guide removes a lot of ambiguity and gives them a way to make sense of all those texts and materials you gave them. If the teachers are more expe-

rienced, the guide gives them a way to stay on track, a measure of accountability you should refer to with them frequently (evaluation time and others)

4. *It enhances parental trust in continuity of a quality program*—Even though very few parents will read through the entire curriculum guide, the parts they become familiar with as their children grow through the grades should be a constant reassurance of why they are in your school. It also tells them:
   - That the quality of your school doesn't just rely on "wonderful" teachers
   - That the pacing and basic elements of their child's education will not be at the mercy of a creative teacher's innovations or lack thereof
   - That the measuring of their student's progress will be objective, based on published standards
5. *It reinforces and integrates naturally with teaching of Scripture*—the key here being natural, because it can and must be. As R. L. Dabney said (in about 1870):

"Every line of true knowledge must find its completeness in its convergency to God, even as every beam of daylight leads the eye to the sun. If religion be excluded from our study, every process of thought will be arrested before it reaches its proper goal. The structure of thought must remain a truncated cone, with its proper apex lacking." Sorry, but there is no published curriculum guide or materials, including ours, that you can buy that will do this for your school and its teachers. Remember, there are no shortcuts to doing this, or anything else, well. But lest you be discouraged, where there used to only be dirt paths, there are now smoother roads to travel. The point here being that teachers need to be *saturated* so thoroughly first in the Word and then in their understanding of their disciplines that the lines Dabney refers to, from true knowledge back to Scriptural principles, are clearly evident to the teacher. Then, in turn, the teacher can make those lines evident, easily, naturally, daily, to the students.

It reinforces a love of the written and spoken word, through a stress on language acquisition (Latin, English, reading, composition)—With the liberty we have to chose our disciplines, knowing they all have their common source in God, we would do well to examine the mechanical means, if you will, that He chose to instruct us. "And the Word became flesh...." "The Word of God is able to instruct the man of God." The Bible contains sixty-six books, a small library. The written and spoken word have exalted positions in the realm of communication from our Creator. Language, and its proper use, should therefore naturally receive a great amount of attention in our schools. So we love books, we love to write, we love to speak well—and we love to help students hone their growing powers of communication.

It doesn't have to respond to fads, trends, but rather reinforces the historical strengths and elements for education—Only since working at Logos have I been introduced to and become familiar with the works of Homer, the history books of Herodotus, the Reformational fathers and their sacrifices, Shakespeare, the framing and compelling issues of our Constitution, and the life of Theodore Roosevelt, to name a few items that were left out of the first seventeen years of my formal education. In our choosing curriculum for these young ones, we would do well to disdain, or at least look very askance at just about anything educationists since Horace Mann have touted. Strength and value take time to be proven. In our choosing and building a curriculum, let's use the following as a three-part litmus test, all understood in the context of biblical definitions:

- Truth—Will we be introducing themes and skills that in some way are timeless, unchanging, have a proven historical value, introduce and support the idea of laws, while making positive use of power? Will we teach the love of truth and the hatred of the false?
- Goodness—In addition to truth, will we choose themes and skills that emphasize the goodness of morality, nobility, heroic acts and purposes? Will we, as part of our work and emphases, teach protocol, manners—love in the details, courtesy and consideration in our schools' atmosphere?
- Beauty—The third test, which adds flavor and loveliness to

the other two, will we seek to use the truly attractive, not flashy or just primary colored? Will we understand and apply the fine arts, emphasizing the goodness of well-trained skills? In a cynical, flat, 2-dimensional age will we introduce the idea of grandeur, through music, and universal, uplifting themes as played out in great dramas?

Guides, like all living things, need maintenance and improvement ideas

It has already been mentioned, but I will say it again—you need to frequently, at least once a year, review the quality and content of your guide. This is done with the invaluable help of your teachers, of course. A few other tips on keeping it current and useful:

1. Make separate guides for elementary and secondary.
2. Establish a board-level curriculum committee with administrators and teachers on it (and the occasional qualified parent. Stick to a set cycle of major discipline reviews (one per year).
3. Use ad-hoc committees for specific research proposals. Here again, qualified parents may be a great help.
4. Devise and distribute an annual form for review and evaluation of the guide by all the teachers.
5. Never settle for mediocre or the status quo; compare the guide constantly to your goals/philosophy.

You may have picked up the idea from the above suggestions that a curriculum committee comprised largely of parents and answerable only to the board is not a good idea. Let me be clear. No, it's NOT a good idea. This isn't a mark against parents involved at this level. It is an admonition to administrators first, then teachers, to lead the way in making, using, and upgrading the school's curriculum guide. If the administrator isn't interested in and excited by the development and improvement of the curriculum ... well, let's just say he might want to check into driving for UPS. Maybe hauling boxes very quickly will give him a charge. He sure shouldn't be leading a classical, Christian school! Enough said.

A very brief note about materials, since you will want to carefully examine your growing options for purchasing:

1. Content philosophy/elements and quality must drive selection, not whether it says its "Christian" on the cover. (You may need to use secular materials.)
2. Are they adaptable to your curriculum?
3. Are they appropriately challenging?
4. Certainly it should be functional, but also as beautiful as possible. Again go for quality. Don't worry about the price tag, just pay for it!
5. Good amount of work for students, not much waste, e.g. lots of white space and/or cutesy graphics.
6. More with less, can they be used for a variety of purposes (integration!).
7. You know, you CAN live without a lot of textbooks. There are other options.

Okay, a few more thoughts about materials from an article I wrote a while back.

NEVER SHOP HUNGRY!

Unlike the early days of our marriage, Julie doesn't send me to the grocery store very often anymore. Perhaps it's because I tend to come home with a few tasty "extras." It is not totally my fault—if I do get sent to the store, it's often on my way home after work and I am ravenous. So, I shop when I'm hungry. Many goodies on the shelf look even better when you're really hungry. The stomach then takes over the rationalizing process normally left to the brain, and lo and behold, I arrive home with olives, peanuts, and other items not on Julie's list.

This analogy seemed to fit a very common situation I frequently hear about through calls from folks inquiring into classical, Christian education—in schools and home schools. One of the first things many people ask me is, "What curriculum/publisher's materials do you use and/or recommend?" Upon inquiring into their situation, I often discover that they are "just beginning" to put together a Christian and classical program and are understandably overwhelmed by the plethora of Christian and secular curricular materials available to them. Which spelling program will be best? How does this math text compare to the one you use? Which Christian publishers do you recommend? These are good and unavoidable questions, but far too often the framework for answering them is absent.

The best and only way to address these questions, and to know how to continue to systematically evaluate curriculum materials in years to come, is to know what you want ahead of time. More specifically, you have to know several related criteria well before you venture into the "grocery stores" of curriculum materials. You don't want to shop too hungry ... so you should know what you are looking for; what's on your list?

What do you want your graduates to "look like" when they are done? What qualities and scholastic training will they have? (Your philosophy applies here!)

What steps (program/course of studies) will you need to construct to prepare your graduates to look the way we want them to? Don't just go "year-to-year" in your planning—set long range goals!

Does your curriculum guide (do you have a guide?) reflect your goals and philosophy?

Those are just a few of the most important questions that, if you know the answers, will greatly assist you in evaluating the relative worth of the multitudinous materials out there. Knowing your educational philosophy ahead of time is like having your shopping list in hand. Your list reflects the menu of meals you plan to serve and now you just need to find the best ingredients at the best price. Just like the grocery stores, publishers of texts and materials (including Logos) want to sell you their products. But they cannot be the best judges of whether their products actually fit your needs. You have to do that.

We have put a lot of work into planning our school and, because not many publishers cater to classical, Christian programs, we have designed lots of our own "ingredients." Many others have found these items helpful since there are growing numbers of Christian educators (home and school) who have a similar philosophy and "shopping list." If this is your situation, we invite you to peruse our shelves. But even here, "never shop hungry!"

A CLASSICAL AND CHRIST-CENTERED COMPUTER EDUCATION?

Not long ago I had a personal harmonic conversion, of sorts. That is, I received two pieces of correspondence at about the same time, and addressing the same subject, only from two completely opposite views. The topic they shared was the use of computers in education. The one strongly advocated our buying into a proposed online classical education. It came by fax, not surprisingly. The other came from *The New York Times.*

"Computers in education," as a concept, is a step beyond the initial concern back in the 80's of "computer education." Computers have become as commonplace in schools as no.2 pencils, if just a tad more expensive to obtain. At Logos we have wrestled with how to approach this overwhelming phenomena ever since the days of buying our first (and only) Atari 400. Do we let this fascinating and growing technology guide our educational philosophy? Will we do the students a disservice in their education by not having cutting-edge equipment in each room? How much should we use computers to teach the students, if at all? Are computers critical or just helpful to a quality education?

The article I received from *The New York Times* said things about using computers in school that I hadn't read or heard anywhere else. It addressed many of those nagging questions with which we wrestle. That being the case, I would like to quote extensively from it:

"Promoted as a solution to the crisis in the classroom, computers have been welcomed uncritically across the educational spectrum. So uncritically that, astonishingly, school libraries, art studios, and music rooms are being replaced by computer labs.

"What's most important in a classroom? A good teacher interacting with motivated students. Anything that separates them—filmstrips, instructional videos, multimedia displays, E-mail, TV, interactive computers—is of questionable value.

"Plop a kid down before such a [computer software education] program, and the message is, 'You have to learn the math tables, so play with this computer.' Teach the same lesson with flash cards, and a different message comes through: 'You're important to me, and this subject is so useful that I'll spend an hour teaching you arithmetic.'

"Computers promise short cuts to higher grades and painless learning. Today's edu-tainment software comes shrink-wrapped in the magic mantra: 'makes learning fun.'

"Equating learning with fun says that if you don't enjoy yourself, you're not learning. I disagree. Most learning isn't fun. Learning takes work. Discipline. Responsibility—you have to do your homework. Commitment from both teacher and student. There's no short cut to a quality education. And the payoff isn't an adrenaline rush, but a deep satisfaction arriving weeks, months, or years later.

"Still, isn't it great that the Internet brings the latest events into the classroom? Maybe. Perhaps some teachers lack information, but most have plenty, thank you. Rather, there is too little class time to cover what's available. A shortage of information is not the problem.

"One of the most common—and illogical—arguments for computers in the classroom is that they'll soon be everywhere, so shouldn't they be in schools? One might as well say that since cars play such a crucial role in our society, shouldn't we make driver's ed central to the curriculum?

"Anyway, computer skills aren't tough to learn. Millions have taught themselves at home. 'In school, it's better to learn how Shakespeare processed words than how Microsoft does.'" [I just love that one!]

In conclusion, Clifford Stoll, the author and a published astrophysicist, by the way, says that excessive reliance on using computers as teachers can encourage the students to assume that "the world is a passive, preprogrammed place, where you need only click the mouse to get the right answer. That relationships—developed over E-mail—are transitory and shallow. That discipline isn't necessary when you can zap frustrations with a keystroke. That legible handwriting, *grammar, analytic thought and human dealings don't matter.*" [My emphasis.]

Looking for simple ways to help in the classroom? Eliminate interruptions from school intercoms. Make classes smaller. Respect teachers.... Protest multiple-choice exams which discourage writing and analytic thinking. If we must push technology into the classrooms, let's give teachers their own photocopiers so they can avoid the long wait at the school copier." [I know I'm going to regret including that last comment!]

Bottom line: We greatly appreciate and use computers at Logos School. But amazingly helpful as it is, even the wonder-tool of the century should be kept subservient to time-tested, good teaching by living and loving teachers. We'll keep running that premise as our main drive.

CHAPTER EIGHT

Daily Management/Programs/Scheduling

When I was in high school (circa early seventies), I would frequently go downtown to buy a new LP (or "record," an antique devise) of a favorite musical group. Upon bringing it home, I naturally wanted to listen to it immediately. However, I very un-naturally wouldn't give myself that pleasure until I had straightened up my bedroom. It wasn't because my mother hounded me or required me to make sure my room was neat before the tunes came on. No, it was just my own strange standard; I couldn't bring myself to listen to a new record in a messy room. It had to be neat or I couldn't relax and enjoy. (Notice I said "neat" and not "clean." That's a different proposition altogether.)

My point here is that, long before I even knew how to spell "administration," I was exhibiting a necessary trait for the job. I would maintain that this trait, maybe not to the bizarre extent I displayed at an early age, should be a natural part of your make-up. You should really like to have a place for everything and, at some point, everything put into its place. True, organizational skills can be learned and should be at least considered, but why would you want to learn them if you didn't have the inclination already? Just for the job? Not a very strong motive to carry you through all the organizational challenges coming your way.

Putting it as simply as possible, since there are lots of advice books on being organized, I would only say here that it's a matter of priority. You begin each day by determining and listing what you *must* do that day (Day-timers are invaluable) and then when you get to the end of day you have a neat list of what you *didn't* get done. Actually, as long as you know what you *should* be spending your time on, anything that trumps that during the day MUST be really important, so you did do your job, after all is said and done.

Your job description will (or should) spell out the practical, daily organizational tasks you will have to oversee. It should include such basic things such as:

- Assigns, oversees room use, set-up, and maintenance.
- Monitors the needs of the school program and solves problems promptly. (That's what is known as a "catch-all" statement.)
- Organizes the various programs for the school (e.g. Speech Meets, Back-to-School Nights, etc.). More on this shortly.
- Supervises ordering of general supplies, textbooks, and equipment.

We have already addressed the supervision of your staff and students on a regular basis. When it comes to the daily organization and management of the school, apart from the people inside it, the two other big areas you will need to pay attention to are Facilities and Finances.

FACILITY MANAGEMENT: i.e. Keeping house

The idea of keeping the "house" neat and clean has to be an attitude as well as a task that virtually all your staff is encouraged to adopt. But in reality it will largely fall on two sets of shoulders—yours and your janitor(s). That piece of trash in the hallway will very likely stay there until one or the other of you actually stop to pick it up and throw it away. How many other people walked by it before you saw it? Probably dozens, including adults. Get used to it. In every home there is only one mom, no matter how many children there are. And no one cares more about the appearance of the home than Mom. YOU are that mom in your school. Whoa. As much as you want and encourage the staff to share that "ownership," plan now to be the one who sees more and acts more than anyone else to see that the place looks good.

But you should make clear delegation to your janitorial staff. My standard line is "If I can see it, you can see it. Therefore, *you* should deal with it before I see it again."

You should also plan to make some guidelines that spell out enforceable standards regarding the facilities. This includes aesthetics, of course. So, for instance, delegate classroom appearance and cleanliness to the teachers and their students. Follow-through with after-school, friendly inspections, with lots of praise for an orderly, clean room. Require the teachers to give you formal, yearly feed-back on what their rooms need. Then respond to their needs, e.g. new carpeting, paint, shelves, etc. Your support of them will lead to their desire to please you and everybody wins.

Use others' eyeballs and ideas. Ask for input from staff and parents regarding the appearance and maintenance of the campus. You can't be omnipresent, believe me. There may be places you don't even see on a weekly basis. It can happen. Therefore, be open to hearing about improvements you know you can't afford. Maybe you can learn something else from the idea. You should be able, when called upon, to list the top five things you would do to make capital improvements to your school. Your board should be informed of your list, by the way, on a semi-regular basis. Even if they don't remember to ask—you still need to let them know. You should also know how much those items will cost, just on the outside possibility that someday there is a fundraiser that takes on one of your priorities.

On a day-to-day basis, I really appreciate it when my teachers tell me (again) about the broken fence or the door that won't shut anymore. It doesn't mean I race off to fix those things, but I try to do something about them right now (write it down, for starters) and put on the janitor's list. The cost of NOT doing something can be high.

A Sad Day

One fall day I was at my desk when Meredith, our kindergarten teacher, dashed into the office. "Tom, a lunch table fell on Brian! I think he's really hurt!"

By that time, I had learned that very few "emergencies" turned out to be worth all the excitement, so I developed the habit of walking, not running when alerted. Panic is easy to instill in kids, and I felt by approaching crises calmly, the kids wouldn't be so upset. However, that day Meredith's face told me running would be very appropriate.

We had purchased several large, fold-up cafeteria tables over time to accommodate the growing number of kids eating at the school. Like all our furniture then, we purchased these six-foot high tables at school auctions. One of the tables had subsequently broken a wheel off, and was not to be used. This day, the table, for some reason, had not been chained against the wall, and was being set up by some of the older elementary kids.

Brian was a first grader. He had been in the lunchroom and had offered the kids his help with the table, Meredith gasped to me as we made our way to the fellowship hall. Another teacher was already with Brian, who lay crying and screaming on the floor. The table had fallen across his lower leg, breaking both bones clear through. That was obvious to the casual observer, which I was anything but ... casual, that is. Brian's leg had a bend in it that hadn't been there before. We called for an ambulance, and a very competent team of EMTs arrived with in what was probably a very brief time normally, but as Brian was screaming the entire time, it seemed to take a few months.

Finally, the team of professionals had Brian ready, and carefully carried him out to the ambulance on a stretcher board.

"Have you contacted his parents? It looks like he may need surgery, so they'll need parental authorization," a blond-headed young man asked me. As a matter of fact we had been repeatedly trying to contact Brian's folks, and had only just discovered that they were in Spokane for the day (eighty miles to the north). Brian was going to have gone home with his pastor's family until evening.

It took a couple of hours, during which Brian lay somewhat sedated, (but not enough to completely remove the pain and moans) before a relative was found who could give the doctors permission to proceed with the surgery. (My, but we were learning all sorts of lessons as a school.)

I called on Brian again later that afternoon, after mentally flagellating myself for: 1) not making sure that stupid table had been better secured or thrown out; 2) for not having a better system in place for obtaining emergency permission; and 3) for allowing this to happen at all! So, in that happy frame of mind I slunk into Brian's room, where he lay with a huge cast up his poor little leg. The pastor's wife, Debbie (who'd been a real trooper all day), was still there, reading to Brian. I came in the hospital room feeling like Admiral Yamamoto should have, had he visited Pearl Harbor the evening of the 7th of December, 1941. Debbie looked up and cheerily announced to Brian:

"Oh look, Brian, here's Mr. Garfield! Isn't this wonderful? It's sort of like Jesus Himself coming to visit you, isn't it!?"

Right. Sigh. What a day.

You get the idea: facility oversight is rather critical.

FINANCES: Keeping the wolf at bay

There are lots of aspects to handling your school's finances. You might not even have to worry about them in your particular role. Maybe your school has a board-appointed treasurer and you just ask him for money and he throws it at you. In any case, I would submit you should have an idea of how your budget works. It is an area fraught with danger and intrigue and your entire constituency will expect you to know a good bit about your school's financial health.

Tuition and Salary Tips

It would be utter folly and a waste of time for any one Christian school administrator to propose a "one-size-fits-all" plan for setting the tuitions and salaries in other schools. Nevertheless, there are some considerations that we all need to ponder as we build these critical financial elements into our growing school's budget. Keep in mind there will always be exceptional circumstances that will need far more thought and planning than the brief ideas here can begin to cover. In our history, we have tried quite a few different arrangements and approaches to charging fees and paying our staff. The following material comes from what we have learned and where we are now. We hope it may be of some help to you.

Tuitions

1. For clarity's sake, "tuitions" in this context means the annual and/or monthly fees parents pay to receive the basic program the school has to offer.
2. Tuitions normally do not include special activity fees, book fees, bus fees, etc. Those types of fees may accompany tuitions on billing, particularly book fees (more on that later), but they normally are user-based and only billed once vs. monthly.
3. Tuitions should comprise the lion's share of the school's revenue, or at least 80%, as a rule of thumb. Less than that and donations or gifts to the school will have to be very large and frequent. You will notice below that 80% of the expense side of the budget is normally payroll. That is rather typical, not a coincidence; your tuitions should cover at least the cost of paying your staff
4. Tuitions are typically billed out on a nine or twelve month basis. The monthly cycle we have preferred is twelve months, July—June, same as our fiscal year. That way the school receives a regular, unbroken monthly revenue. Most parents like it because the amount is lower per month and they can just figure it as part of their year-round bills, vs. nine "heavy" months, and three "light" ones.
5. It is not a good idea to raise tuitions much more than about 5% a year. This has been demonstrated by the experiences of a good number of Christian schools. More than that and parents worry that this will be a trend. Less than that and you won't be able to put much into raising salaries or paying for new books.

6. If you are just starting out, it would be a good idea to research the tuition amounts of other local private schools. You can bet the parents of your school will do that. Then determine where your salaries will be set and your total payroll. Again, that will be your largest expense. After payroll, your overhead can be fairly accurately calculated by some careful checking into materials and facility costs.
7. Some schools charge two additional fees related to tuitions—registration and book fees. A significant registration fee is a good idea because it encourages the parents to seriously consider your school before seeking entry. Registration fees should be non-refundable (as should all fees after the start of your fiscal year), like earnest money on a house purchase. Therefore, if they back out at the last minute, the parents stand to lose a fair amount of money. If there is no penalty of sorts for backing out, families will do just that, and your budget can be severely damaged.
    - Book fees can be appropriate at the secondary level (7th-12th grades) where text costs are very high. (It is very typical for classical schools to use college-level texts that are extremely expensive). The downside to separate book fees is that parents don't like to be hit with lots of different fees as they begin the school year. It may be better to just count the registration fee income toward text purchases, or charge enough in the tuition payments to pay for salaries and materials.
8. A final consideration, for now, on tuitions. It is very important to make it clear to the parents that the cost you are charging is for a year's education. They should know that you have contracted with the teachers for a year, and purchased materials for the year. When families leave during the year, they often don't realize the impact this has on your budget. Not surprisingly, they assume the school is like any other service they contract for on a monthly basis, like the

phone company. When they stop phone services, that's it. But when they stop paying the school after only two months, you are still obligated to pay the teacher the same amount for the year, you have already paid for books and supplies, and you may have turned down a student who would have stayed for the year. Some schools have required families to pay either the whole amount or one semester's worth up front, to offset any financial loss should the family leave. We have not done this, but we do let families know that *all* fees are non-refundable, including advance fees paid for the year (which we offer a discount for paying up front).

Salaries

As with all aspects of your school, you want to ensure you have Scriptural principles for all you do. The Bible is not silent about paying employees.

1. The first principle to note here is that the laborer is worthy of his wages. If you hire them, pay them appropriately. In our situations, that means researching the market value (as being set by ACCS schools, not the government schools) of your teachers and set your salaries as close as possible to that value.

2. Related to that same principle, it is not advisable to set different salary amounts for the same tasks. In other words, pay single women and married men the same amount if they have the same type and amount of work. This may sound politically correct, but it's just the right thing to do. Needs certainly vary, but seek other means to help staff members who may want to earn more. Benefits can be of more help to families than single folks, e.g. tuition discounts for half- and full-time work. There may be additional tasks that heads of households could do for compensation. Coaching, bus driving, etc. may work out. Another avenue may be in the area of constructing curriculum materials the school could use and receiving a merit increase for those items or work.

3. Another biblical principle is that you don't withhold pay when it is in your power to pay. Now, that seems obvious. Why would you withhold pay? How about if you have a huge utility bill or mortgage payment, money is low, and both payday and those bills are due on the same day? You only have enough money to pay either payroll or the bills. What do you do? Answer: You pay your staff and, assuming your board has given prior approval, you contact the companies you owe, tell them how much you can pay and ask what arrangements you can make with them. That is an extremely awkward and humbling situation. To help avoid this kind of thing, by the way, consider establishing a Contingency Fund to help with cash flow problems. Also, insist that your families pay on time and in full.

4. In constructing a salary schedule, you will want to build in raises, usually based on longevity. If a person has done a good job for you, you want to keep them, as well as show them you appreciate their work. That means a raise. DO NOT set arbitrary salary amounts each year. Your staff should know what they can expect if they stay for five more years, earn another degree, or assume more responsibility, all based on set figures, not your personal whims. There should be a difference in pay among the various jobs in the school reflecting the difficulty and responsibility level of the tasks involved. For example, the administrator should receive the highest salary; no apologies or explanations should be needed. Secondly, the teachers' salary schedule should be constantly reviewed by the board to determine how much and often the entire schedule can be cranked up. Put simply, it is probably not possible to pay your teachers too much. Unlike the pagan teachers' unions, your teachers won't complain and whine for more pay, but they do some of the best work possible on God's earth and for His kingdom.

5. Next you should have separate and lower pay schedules for secretarial and support personnel. They should receive a livable wage, but they rarely have to take work home (as the teachers do), and it is far easier to find a good secretary than a good teacher. (Parents love to do some of those support tasks—librarian, secretary, etc.)
6. *Benefits* are a major consideration. Typically a staff benefits package at schools like ours include any or all of the following:
   - *Tuition breaks* for school-age staff children. We use either 100% discounts for full-time and 50% for half-time respectively. If they work more than half, but less than full, we still give a 50% discount on fees. This benefit should be accompanied by the policy requirement to have the school-age children of staff members attend your school, You can probably figure out a good reason for that requirement.
   - *Retirement co-pay*. This is good to encourage longevity, so make a schedule of increasing co-pay amounts each year. Your married men will particularly appreciate this. This should be a pre-tax deduction; check it out.
   - *Workman's compensation*. This covers any injuries your staff may suffer while on the job. Usually this is required by law anyway, but it is inexpensive, relatively, and in some states even pays back dividends for safe work records.
   - *Continuing education*. This should be a line-item in the budget in any case, for on-site training of the staff. But you should also have money available (and approval procedures) for staff members to get financial help in obtaining an advanced degree, college courses, or ACCS certification, going to ACCS conferences or other appropriate training.
   - *Medical health insurance*. What a pain this area can be!

(Pun intended.) But you should consider it carefully since medical costs are so incredibly high, and you're going to be asked about it by potential employees. We haven't found any group plans everyone likes, SO We have gone with a set amount of monthly pay designated for just the staff member's premium. They pay extra for their dependents to the company of their choice. It is my belief that every insurance company is as reliable and worthwhile as a gambling casino, so let the buyer beware. You might seriously consider the growing number of Christian cooperative medical payment programs. Again, let the buyer beware, but at least you are helping someone else with your monthly payments, and not throwing the money into someone's already burgeoning assets.

7. As noted in the tuitions section above, your payroll area should account for about 80% of your total budgeted expenses. More than that and your overhead is being impinged—you may be tempted to spend too little and buy inferior supplies and materials. Less than that and you probably won't have enough to construct a workable salary schedule and benefits package.

As the Word says, money can be the source of all sorts of problems, even sins. Seek godly counsel as you set tuitions and salaries. Keep the communications open with your parents and staff as you set these amounts (not seeking a democratic support), and they will normally go along if they understand what is happening and why. Your board should be your primary support in all these matters. Keep accountable to those folks and the trust that is so necessary in handling money will be easier to maintain.

Ye Ol' Food Shelf

Since we (the teachers) didn't have salaries in our early years, one of the ways parents contributed to ease the financial lacks of the staff was through the "food shelf." In a room off the church kitchen, which we eventually adopted for everything from home economics classes to typing, a large metal rack of shelves was placed. Parents encouraged each other to keep it stocked with food stuffs and dry goods the teachers could then take home. This was a very welcome relief, especially to the few married staff members we attracted in the early years. The single staff members liked it, too. At times it was a little awkward, though, such as when a large delivery of goods would come. Married guys, like myself, would try to think like our wives and take the right (that is, boring) items, instead of just loading up on chocolate chips and cases of pop. The differences between married and single people were obvious to the casual observer at the food shelf. Everyone would try to be polite, and let the others take as much as they needed. "No, you go ahead and take that last bag of sugar", some married guy would say to a single gal, "my family of nine doesn't need sugar." Or the single gal saying, "Are you sure you don't want this bag of Oreo's?" "Ah, uh, no, no, thanks anyway", the married guy says, drool running down his tie.

A few items would stay on the shelves for weeks. I distinctly remember wondering why some otherwise caring parent would purchase a tin of canned oysters! It stayed there for months. Who knows? It may still be there.

The following is submitted for your consideration only. It is certainly not the only or best plan, but it works.

ANNUAL BUDGET DEVELOPMENT PROCESS—One model

PREPARATIONS: Prior to any specific budget planning by the superintendent, he is to meet with the appropriate board-appointed finance committee to solicit board and/or committee input and recommendations. Review of any adopted and active Five-year Goals should be done at this time. After the first draft of the budget is completed, it should be presented to the finance committee for comments and proposed revisions. This will also give the superintendent a "feel" for the board's reaction to the proposed budget.

(Some of the following steps may be done concurrently, not necessarily consecutively.)

1. Determine previous salary schedule/benefits and any proposed revisions for the coming year.
2. Determine potential new staffing positions (check with all appropriate administrative personnel for input on needed positions) and accompanying salaries.
3. Construct anticipated payroll based on 100% retention of current staff + new positions + additional benefits.
4. Distribute and collect up-to-date surveys for budget requests and assessments from staff members.
5. Summarize surveys and review as necessary with other concerned administrative staff.
6. Review currently budgeted OE (Operating Expenses) and determine the stability of current budget amounts based on actual costs to date (from Budget Reports-YTD).
7. Anticipate differences in areas requiring more funding for the coming year and those areas of relative stability in costs. Project both into new budget.
8. Create new accounts for any needed delineation of new expenditures.
9. Set OE costs for the coming year based on anticipated payroll, survey requests, and overhead.
10. Anticipate enrollment figures, set tuition increases, discount schedules, gift income (development financial goals). Determine actual per-student income based on 90% of new fee amount per-student.
11. Go over proposed new budget with all other administrators, development officers, and finance committee members. Consider all acquired input and make any necessary revisions.
12. Present balanced budget to the school board no later than regularly scheduled meeting in March for its review and final adoption. Communicate highlights to parents.

A number of private schools get in trouble each year for not paying attention to some of the basic ideas below. These were constructed one year by and for Logos School, based on material provided by an inspection of our operations by a local CPA. I hope you find it helpful.

LOGOS SCHOOL FINANCIAL INTERNAL CONTROLS

PURPOSE

To define and standardize the primary means of processing funds coming into or going out of Logos School and who is responsible for each step of the process.

TUITION BILLING:

- Superintendent recommends fee schedule.
- School Board approves fee schedule (in annual budget).
- Families may choose 9, 10, 11, or 12 month billing.
- Bookkeeper makes up, records, and sends monthly statements, normally July through June.

RECEIVING CASH/CHECKS FOR TUITION/GIFTS:

- Front office secretary receives monies from person or in daily mail. She issues receipts for cash and as requested. She immediately endorses all checks for deposit and places them in a locked cash box.
- Bookkeeper picks up all monies from cash box to be deposited; processes all funds as appropriate to computerized accounts; constructs general account bank deposit summaries and slips (recording names and purpose).
- Secretary makes actual deposit to bank.

INTERNAL HANDLING OF MONIES AND TUITION ACCOUNTS:

- Secretary keeps superintendent's signature stamp in a locked box.
- All unused checks will be stored in a locked cabinet.
- Secretary oversees control of the petty cash box.

- Bookkeeper credits payments (from deposits), pre-approved adjustments to customer accounts and assesses any late fees.
- Bookkeeper prepares A/R reports as requested by superintendent. Also files written statements on all tuition fee adjustments which have been approved and signed by superintendent.
- Bookkeeper reconciles bank statements monthly.
- Development secretary takes all gift checks out of cash box; makes photocopies of check, constructs a gift deposit summary and deposit slip. Copy of summary is given to bookkeeper, deposit is given to front office secretary to be taken to bank.
- Development secretary fills out receipts for all gift income, and gives to development director.

EXPENDITURES FROM SCHOOL CHECKING

- Superintendent recommends annual expenses in annual budget.
- School board approves planned expenses, as per adopted budget.
- Materials and services not contracted out (contracted services would include phone, gas, electric, etc.) will require superintendent's approval prior to commitment of funds.
- If a major purchase or service is necessary, approval must be given by superintendent and an order is given to bookkeeper to inform of upcoming expense.
- Bookkeeper alerts superintendent if applicable account is over budget or in danger of being so. Superintendent decides whether to go ahead with purchase.
- After order is received, originator (applicable staff member) checks contents against original order. If correct, invoice and/or packing slip goes to book-keeper, verifying status of contents and charges.

- Bookkeeper checks invoice against p.o. and statements against invoices, and twice monthly prepares checks (requiring two signatures) for payment.
- With accompanying invoices, superintendent, or approved staff member, and other approved signatory sign checks for payment.
- Bookkeeper prepares for mailing and secretary mails.
- Bookkeeper prepares A/P reports for superintendent as requested.
- Superintendent approves all summer projects; then bookkeeper is given description of project, cost estimate, funding source and person in charge of project.

SPECIAL PROGRAMS/EVENTS

Question : How many times does it take to begin a tradition in a small classical, Christian school? Answer: Just one! So, as the old knight in Indiana Jones movie said, "Choose wisely!" And, in a converse correlation, it seems that the easier it is to start a tradition, the harder it is to stop. In other words, what you begin may last for a lonnnggg time.

At the risk of making you sick of hearing (or reading) it, EVERY program you chose should have a direct, thought-out connection to your school's ... ready? ... Yes, **philosophy**! Therefore, a brief look at some categories and principles you may want to consider:

Not All Special Days Are Alike

Holi—(Holy) Days—It should be plain to all concerned what the purpose of these events is: typically, they are to recall and/or recognize events which are:

Biblically emphasized as of primary importance to the Church, e.g. Christmas, Good Friday, Easter

Recognized by the historical Christian Church as of first importance, e.g. Reformation Day

Days of Remembrance: Recall, recognize significant events which are:

Consistent with qualities the Bible upholds, e.g. honor, truth, goodness, beauty, courage, etc.

Historically critical to an understanding of western civilization.

Keys to understanding our past and current American culture.

Related to individuals who, individually or collectively, exemplify biblical characteristics and have achieved noteworthy accomplishments. Suggestions for this category would include: Presidents' Day, Memorial Day, Thanksgiving, Columbus Day, birthdays of people like Theodore Roosevelt, Robert E. Lee, George Washington Carver, Booker T. Washington, Thomas "Stonewall" Jackson, John Winthrop, Martin Luther, certain missionaries, etc.

ACADEMIC/CULTURAL: Organize events which

Reinforce, encourage review of knowledge taught, e.g. spelling bees, math competitions, trivia contests

Recognize and practice skills we value, e.g. speech meets, oral competitions, debates

Reinforce cultural or aesthetic standards, e.g. Knights' festival (several days of celebrations in a medieval fashion—food, dancing, sword fights, speeches, etc.), Protocol nights (prior training in etiquette, then an evening in formal attire at a dinner, then a symphony or play), concerts, plays

Honor and inform family members, e.g. Grandparents' Day, Open House, Back-to-School

Then there's just the pragmatic side of things to consider. Or in administrative parlance, **logistical considerations**, such as staffing, time, and place. You will need to carefully consider the impact of the program on:

Your staff—The best people for organizing a consistent, high-quality program (that needs someone other than you to organize it) will be a staff person. However, be careful not to take advantage of their being close at hand. Be generous with any compensation (if money is tight, give some time off as a reward) and be mindful of their other duties.

Timing—You'll need to have an eye out for not only possible calendar or timing conflicts with your own schedules, but also what might be happening in the community, the churches, and nationally. One night many, many years ago, unbeknownst to me, I scheduled a parent meeting night on the evening when M.A.S.H. was having its final show on TV. Big surprise, few people came. It wasn't until later I heard the main reason. "Sheesh!" was my general reaction then and, having seen the episode not long ago, now as well.

Place—Unless you have your own facility, and sometimes even then, you need to plan WAY ahead to make sure you have the space and place you need. (Once I had to change a Christmas program date because I hadn't let our Activities Director know and he had already scheduled a basketball game in the gym for that night.) If you're renting or borrowing a place, see it for yourself, don't just go by descriptions. Keep in mind who is attending the event so you know what you'll need for parking, accessibility (grandparents?), lighting, sound, seating, etc. Food is always a pain to organize, but almost always a sure draw, too. So, the place will need to be able to accommodate the food needs.

By the way, just a hint on getting an audience, presupposing you want one: Involve the *students* as much and wherever possible. You get the kids and the parents will follow, to put it crassly. But just as with your staff, be mindful of how much time and how often you are asking the students to do things outside of school work.

Sample Yearly Special Events/Programs/Holidays

The following list of events, holidays, and programs is not meant to be comprehensive. New ideas may and should be introduced at any time. These are some typical programs, holidays, etc., that our school has done or not done, which can also be significant as a message, too.

"*Examine everything; hold fast to that which is good.*" (I Thes.5:21)

EVENT	TIMING	ACTIVITIES
Staff Orientation	Late Aug	2-3 days of staff training
Parent Orientation	Late Aug	New family info night
Back-To-School Night	Late Sept	Parents meet w/teachers for planning
Birthdays Of Historical People (e.g. T.Roosevelt, Robert E. Lee, George Washington Carver, etc.)	As noted on calendar	For instruction on significance
Reformation Day	Oct 30	Some basic instruction on event and people
Thanksgiving	Late Nov	Normally two and half days off. Major emphasis. Education on historical and biblical purpose of holiday.
Speech Meets	Late Nov	In-school and inter-school
Christmas	Dec 25	Normally two weeks off. Major emphasis on Christ's birth and mission. Special evening program.
Knights Festival	Jan	Grades 7-12, days of feasts, oral competitions, sword fights, dancing, posters, etc., for school spirit
Spelling Bees	Feb	In-school and inter-school
Presidents' Day	Mid-Feb	(Mon) One day off. Encourage knowledge of Washington & Lincoln
Protocol Nights	Mar/Apr	"Low"(9th/10th) & "High" (11th/12th) evening out
Knights Day	Fri before break	Mini conference for secondary
Spring Break	Mid-March	One week off
Good Friday/ Resurrection Day (Easter)	Mar/Apr	Special assembly Th aft., Friday off
Standardized Testing	Mid-April	Standardized testing of 1st-11th
Grandparents' Day/ Talent Night	Late April	Grandparents visit elem. classes, evening program
Open Houses/Concerts	Spring	Displays, evening program
Field Day	Next to last day	Elem students clean in AM, play in PM
8th Grade Promotion	Last Wed	Evening to honor transition to HS
Awards Assemblies	Last day	Year-end awards for elementary/secondary
High School Graduation	Last Sat	High school evening ceremony
ACCS Natl Conference	Late June	Logos teachers as instructors/attendees
Teacher Training	Mid-July	Five day training for classical, Christian teachers, hosted/ conducted by Logos School

In our early years, each program, assembly, and event was like a wedding—loads of sweat-filled days of preparation, the pulse-racing event itself, and then ... it's over. Even the kids got nervous sometimes, too. But it was the adults, parents and teachers, who really did the nail-biting, and agonizing over each aspect of a program. The presentation-style programs like the ones for Christmas, Thanksgiving, Science and Art Fairs, or the bane of many teachers' existence—assemblies, were the hardest on the teachers. It was the teachers who had to coordinate every detail to make it look as smooth as a Broadway production. But the competition-style programs, such as the speech meets or spelling bees were death on the parents. The teachers often suffered in silence, bearing their load with a stiff upper lip, sort of like the Brits during the Battle of Britain. The parents, on the other hand, bless 'em all, felt under no such stoic obligation.

The day before or after a competitive event, I was sure to hear from at least one mother with a "concern" ... "Tom, I don't mean to complain, but about the spelling bee yesterday...."

"Yes, your daughter did very well, didn't she?!"

"Well ... she did, I guess, but did you know that she had a cold? And that the word she got wrong was one she's had trouble with all year, and ... I know you didn't mean to do this, but you had her sit in the very same spot on the stage she sat in last year. You know how those little things can throw off a child's concentration. Is there a rule about mixing the order of the students each year? Maybe you could draw names from a hat or something. That might have helped her have the confidence to get first place instead of second. What do you think?"

"Gee, honey, can we discuss this at home? I'm kind of busy right now."

Actually Julie never has called me about such an absurd concern at work. She has been really good to wait until I did get home.

First Graduation

Certainly one of the proudest and happiest days we enjoyed was the day in late May, 1985. That was the day we held our first high school graduation! Jim Quist had been our oldest student to come to the school our first year. At that time he was in ninth grade, the youngest son of Shirley Quist, one of our founding board members. Jim was a very pleasant and bright young man who was top of his class for all four years of high school; in fact he was the only one in his class for all four years, but the point still stands. Jim didn't even have anyone near his age until he was a senior. That was the year Eric came as our only junior.

The younger students naturally looked up to and admired Jim. Thankfully, he always gave them good reason to do so. But it wasn't all a bed of roses, or perhaps it was, as long as you recall that thorns play a role in such a picture. Jim was a normal young man who at times longed for the company of other students his age, and opportunities we could not provide. For example, he and I both knew my offers to let him be quarterback on our high school football team didn't carry a lot of conviction. We had a number of long talks, and no doubt he and his folks did too, during those four years. But he stuck it out and his teachers enjoyed tutoring him immensely. Where possible, we taught him with some of the younger secondary students as they came along. But by and large he was on his own.

That's why that first graduation day meant a great deal to everyone in the school. Jim was graduating! He had made it, and Lord willing, there would be many more to follow him. His mom and the other older students, especially Beth (of the broken leg) who was three years his junior, had a great time decorating the church sanctuary for the evening ceremony. Beth also made sure she got to narrate a slide-show history of Jim's life, before and during Logos. The entire school board, and most of the student body (about one hundred and twenty by then) was there to recognize Jim's accomplishment. We sang "O The Deep, Deep Love of Jesus," the hymn chosen by the class of 1985. Jim gave a valedictorian address, which was fully earned in every way. He had truly earned it, in spite of the lack of any competition. (We didn't, however, have him do the salutatorian address.)

Don and Shirley Quist, and Jim's teaching sister, Debbie, sat in the front pew of the church sanctuary and just about glowed with pride. Jim humbly took in all the praise and attention, including a medallion as the first graduate of Logos School.

Afterwards we held a reception for him in the fellowship hall downstairs. He commented on some of the many memories he would take with him to college (where he had received a honor's scholarship for being first in his class, really!).

CHAPTER NINE

Development/Community Relations

There were many aspects of administrative work that I was clueless about when we began. To be concise, just about all of them! I can easily recall those first days of religiously listening to ACSI-provided cassette tapes about starting a Christian school. But even those didn't touch on the aspect of development, or as some folks think of it, fundraising. (There is much more to it than that, which I will address shortly.) Considering that our financial structure was, shall we say, a bit unusual as we began, gift income was very critical since it was what our staff lived on! I believe our initial approach was along the lines of George Muller who told no one but God about his orphanage's needs. God honored that approach and blessed in amazing ways. Along the way, though, we came to discover, mostly by reading the Word, that it isn't wrong to let other saints know of certain, appropriate needs. (For instance, Paul's letter to the Romans could be considered, at least in part, a fundraising letter.) Not to mention raising tuitions to that we could actually put together a real salary schedule.

In any event, we came to see the value and need for enlightening and encouraging the folks who knew about Logos to consider supporting us financially. How to do that biblically and tactfully? Well, let's define our terms first, so we know what it is we are trying to do.

So, what are we talking about with "Development?"

Well, since you're reading this, I will give you a rough-and-ready definition:

"Development" within the context of a Christian school, concerns itself with the overall reputation the school engenders among its various constituencies. The goal being to foster such an accurate, well-respected reputation that more and more people will come to regard supporting the school financially as a wise investment.

That's actually not too bad of a definition, if I do say so myself. I chose words that carry a lot of significance and require some examination. (By the way, I have included some documents on the Development Officer's job in the appendix, so I will limit what I say here.) Consider the meanings of "reputation," "constituencies," "accurate, well-respected," and "investment." Certainly, the bottom line is that you want folks to fork over bucks to your school. Fine. But if that's all you want or even make that your primary objective, I would submit you will not only fail to realize your objective, you will miss many other blessings. Again, consider the words I used and their application in our settings:

Reputation—Our Lord said to be wary when all men speak well of you. Put another way, if everyone says your school's great, two things at least are happening: 1) Someone's lying, and 2) You probably aren't doing your job very well.

The very nature of what we're about should cause some folks to be thrilled and other folks to be dismayed. Don't get me wrong, your school's reputation is a valuable commodity definitely. That, too, is scriptural. We are to consider how we are perceived by the world as we do the Lord's work, so that His Name is not tarnished by our foolishness. Rather, it should be exalted by our good works. A good name and reputation require consistent, hard work, doing for your parents what you said you'd do. They will spread the word, believe me. But still, some will be pleased with your school and some won't, even though both groups see your good works. The out-working of the gospel has that affect—it attracts some and it repels others.

Constituencies—Think of all the categories of folks your school includes just by existing: Families, alums, grandparents, extended family members—aunts, uncles, etc., family friends, churches, local business people, public school officials and teachers, other private schools, homeschoolers, possibly university groups (as we have in our town), and local government officials. That's probably an incomplete list, but you get the idea. There are a LOT of people watching your little school, and they all have varying views, most of them either somewhat inaccurate or at least uninformed to some degree. They ALL need to be informed to some extent about the nature and purpose of your work. "Why do we have another private school in our area, anyway?" many locals will naturally ask. Part of the Development Officer's work is to aide you in answering that question. And you have to answer it constantly since the community members constantly change. This is necessary long before they will even think about possibly helping you financially.

Accurate, well-respected—As I just alluded to, giving all those people an accurate, that is, truthful and clear, picture of your school's work is going to take a lot of work and a good bit of time. A good reputation, someone said, takes a long time to build and a moment to lose. Sad, but true. So, you want to enlighten as many as possible about the unique nature of your school, all the while working hard to fulfill your goals within the school. Here's a strange fact—you will make a better reputation for your school by NOT going with what seems popular, but by sticking to your philosophic guns. Even the pagans understand a weak-kneed, spineless organization when they see one. Even if they disagree or even hate your reason for existing, they can't help but respect you for being honest in all your dealings and basically doing what you say you're going to do, educationally. When your grads start showing up in colleges and local work places, your reputation will have faces and voices.

Investment—Whoever does your development work (get someone full-time as SOON as possible!) has to understand and love the fact that a gift to your school is unlike almost any other giving. Every gift is nothing less than an investment in the lives of your students. Sadly that sounds overused and cliched, but we need to show the direct connection. Think about it, our funding should come from two main sources—tuitions from satisfied parents and gifts from impressed donors. Both sources rely on seeing the connection between their money, their investment, and the benefit to the students they know or know about. This requires that your development person is also clearly interested in *people,* not their checkbooks. The message will become clear—every single person who works for your school is interested in God's work in people, whether it's the students or the folks who have faithfully given regularly to help the school. A great example of this is the way our development officer is regarded by our donors. He has visited ill grandparents in the hospital, and not with his hand out. He has sent birthday cards to alums, chatted with businessmen, and called long distance donors just to say hello. He invests in people, therefore, many of those people invest in Logos because of his example and living representation of what we are about.

Some practical points

*Gifts or donations can either be undesignated (general) or designated. That is, they can be used as the school sees fit or they can be used only as the donor designates. The distinction is important and must be acknowledged. Heaven help you if you use designated gifts for something other than what the donor desired. That is a violation of trust. Big mistake.

*General gifts should not exceed about 20% of your budgeted revenue. Tops. That's not just me saying so, that's a somewhat proven standard. More than that and you run the real risk of not making budget. Less than that is fine, of course.

*When (hopefully not IF) you get a development officer, he should be paid a set salary, not a portion or percentage of the gifts he raises. Think about it. Why do so many folks get grossed out by car salesmen? Okay, other than the fact that they often have the personality of carnival ride operators? It's at least partly because everyone knows this guy is going to get paid more if he sells me this car! You DON'T want your development officer viewed that way. Or for him to have that attitude. Again, this is an industry standard, if you will. But lots of Christian schools, even classical ones, think it would be an incentive to the development guy to have to get paid from his "sales." Yuck.

*Grant-writing is way over-blown, in my opinion. Yes, your D.O. (if I may) should know where to look and how to write for a grant from a reputable foundation. But from what we have found and observed in other schools, IF you get the grant (for which much time and paperwork was spent), it is almost always for a specific, capital acquisition or project. Science is currently a popular theme for which funding is available. That's great ... for that limited purpose. My two cents would be not to encourage your D.O. to spend a lot of time on grant-writing. The returns from spending the lion's share of his time fostering relations with donors are much greater and longer lasting in their benefits to the school.

*Don't "nickle-and-dime" people to death. Only invest the time and effort into a worthwhile fundraiser. Frankly, car washes, bake sales and candy drives are maybe OK for a class project or trip, but not for the school as a whole. I can't count how many times, since I've had four children go through Logos, we parents have paid for (and even made) the pies that we later buy back at an evening event. Sincerity is fine and necessary, but consider what is being said about the school and what it considers worthwhile. Instead, auctions, tasteful banquets and the like are not only a higher class event, but they will bring in more money.

*As your school grows and your secondary (especially) wants to do fundraisers for this or that, it is absolutely imperative that the Development Officer be informed and listened to. He should coordinate events, date-wise, so there are no embarrassing double-bookings, or worse, a really dumb fundraising programs. (And there are a plethora of dumb programs out there! We were offered the opportunity to sell tiny bottles of "actual" Jordan River water for a profit as a fundraiser in our early years. Really! And you want to know the real discouraging aspect? It didn't even cure leprosy!)

*Our Development Director, Ed Van Nuland, has written a wonderful handbook on the whole area of Development. Obviously I would strongly recommend you get a copy of your own.

CHAPTER TEN

Growth

As the Lord blesses your "house" (otherwise you build in vain, right?), you will see growth. Growth in enrollment (remember, you are offering water to some very thirsty people), growth in budgets, growth in facilities and staffing, and most importantly, growth in the school's overall program maturation. That should be evident in the way the board makes decisions (wise and informed), the way the school culture reflects the look and spirit of antithesis to our popular culture, and everywhere in the school there is a godly, joyful aspect. Maturity will be reflected in the kinds of families you attract over time and the length of time they stay with you. Your reputation in the community should mature, which means many businesses and folks will be glad you are there. Possibly (and likely) others may become more vocal in their desire that you NOT be there, or that you at least conform to their worldview.

So, much like marriage and raising kids, the life cycles schools experience have common phenomena—learning and growing through trials, taking advantage of opportunities, but mostly staying the original course. But there will be more and more times that you are tempted to ask yourselves "Why are we seeing what we are seeing now?" And "Is this the end or is there any hope?" Of course there's hope. Nothing is impossible with God.

Referring back again to those life cycles I mentioned, below are some very likely scenarios you may experience shortly after your first year or two (see the ***Growth Cycle Chart*** in the Appendix of Documents).

Third Year Pattern

**First Two Years*—First year, you fall off one side of the horse, and then the second year you fall off the other side, trying to correct first year mistakes. It's almost unavoidable. The trick is to stay humble enough and hard-working enough to make changes for third year.

**Third Year Stride*—This is especially true in teaching, but also in the school. Whatever you do for three years will be considered virtually sacrosanct, particularly by the kids, and therefore by the parents, too. Now is a good time to do some self-examination of critical areas (board and admin). Trends can be spotted by now, such as, are you paying all your bills, on time? It's a good idea. Are your families satisfied that you are doing what you said you would do for their kids? Perhaps it's time to think about extra-curricular programs. Or time to eliminate some of the more burdensome programs. (We waited about fifteen years before we shot our Fall Carnival down. It had gone from great parent help and leadership to just the poor teachers making up the booths. Zap!) Talk to a number of key families, some who've been with you since you began and some who've just joined. Try to assess their satisfaction levels. Discuss your findings with the board and compare where you are with where you wanted to be.

Signs that tell you when the "honeymoon" is over (which is normal and right)

This comes after the first flush of excitement, when it was hard work, yes, but everyone was so involved and you heard lots of optimistic views, many encouraging comments from parents. That's what I am calling the "honeymoon period." Then, to extend the metaphor, comes the work of the "marriage" and the seeming reduction in the "romance"....

**Parents—Excitement level seems to drop, PTF lethargy sets in, gener-*

al involvement declines—The bloom is off the rose, people only seem to want to talk about problems, and not show up for general meetings or projects. Welcome to legitimacy. It's not necessarily bad. In some ways it can be a good sign—silence can be golden. Contented people don't come and tell you they are content. They just are.

**Staff-Energy and zeal seem to wane, but it's more likely just maturity; changing needs (more money!), benefits desired*—Our record of hiring for the first number of years reads like a Who's-Who of single people. It seemed like we had a revolving front door. The young married types were not much better when it came to longevity. "Hey, surprise, guess who's pregnant?" You want to mature to hiring older, possibly more experienced folks. Parents are best, remember? They will bring a different kind of zeal that lasts, along with just more maturity. But they will certainly need more tangible support and benefits. At times you will feel that you are trying to develop a champagne program on a beer budget, especially with regard to staffing. Relax, you are. Be patient and trust, He does own the cattle on well more than a thousand hills.

**Board—Changing policy needs, vision differences (cracks) appear, personalities vs. common good become more manifest*—At first, there was this good will, an *esprit de corps,* and a seemingly common desire to get any water after being in the desert, then ... constant, nit-picking clarifications on policies. Discussions start to bring out underlying vision differences, in curriculum especially. "Why don't we make this easier?" Or "We need to push these kids harder, up the ante!" It's a very common affliction—starting personalities and desires giving way, others not seeking the common good, or new board members who are not aware of the school's history and starting vision. Remember, educating the board is a non-stop job for you, particularly. But you still might lose even some founding board members. That's very painful, but keep focused and humble.

**Students—Begin to desire a school identity, more recognition of grade placement, more interesting programs*—After the first possibly rather compliant bunch of students, you may start getting kids who want and expect the school to look and be like a "school." Again, that's not all bad, it can be a catalyst to good and necessary changes. It's amazing how quickly we can get used to the same ol' thing and not even see opportunities for delightful improvements. As your school develops a full K-12 program, the older students will want to be seen and identified as being older, not just a tag-on to the elementary grades. That's a legitimate concern and desire. Maturity and accomplishment should be recognized and encouraged. Find practical ways to separate the older students from the elementary, plan events for only the secondary, require a different look in dress, give them responsibilities and privileges that the younger students will see and yearn to obtain when they get there. Then, when the older students DO interact with the younger, as you want them to, there will be a real, recognized distinction and the younger ones will be thrilled to have such older, mature students talking with them!

Significant dangers accompanying growth

Cancer grows; so do weeds and pond scum. Unguided or quality growth is not always pretty, even though numbers can be very alluring. You have worked hard to attract folks, yet you can (but shouldn't) be swayed or driven off course by growth. This is directed toward those who make direction decisions about your school. And remember, YOU are the lighthouse keeper!

**Drift factor*—Many pressures come to bear—bills, facility needs/requirements, special requests by families, hiring needs (the temptation toward snob appeal is strong in our classical world, but master's degrees are not the be-all, end-all), community regard, Christian community regard (you know which churches, particularly). All can, and if you are not diligent, will push you off course. How do you recognize the pushing? Listen to what these folks are saying.... Does your vision seem a bit "unrealistic" or is it just being called that? Compare it to sister schools of greater longevity—use the strength of comrades in arms, don't listen to those who may not be your friends (read Ezra and Nehemiah for examples of sticking to your guns). Some other "pushing" indicators:

**Back to Egypt noises*—The Israelites waffled and whined, even after seeing God's amazing miracles of deliverance up close. ("Egypt" in this case, lest you miss the great analogy, can be government education or possibly modern, aimless Christian education—both fit rather well.)

How do modern "Israelites" (parents, board members) sound? At the first, second or more signs of problems/struggles.... "Golly! This is hard work! Maybe we shouldn't have come out into this desert of classical ed. Maybe we should turn back into a 'normal' Christian school!" Individual parents will talk that way every year, but board-level discussion shouldn't descend to that level.

**Party spirit*—One of the nastiest afflictions that comes with a widening influence and a modicum of success—board members with agendas or party platforms who start talking as though they represent a certain portion of school families, instead of all of them. "Danger, danger, Will Robinson!" (From *Lost In Space*, for all you non-boomers!)

**Professional pride*—This can afflict even the youngest school, and the newest staff member, i.e. the temptation to act/think as though "we're the professionals." The parents are obviously a bunch of ignorant busybodies who aren't letting us do our work! Hey, if the government school teachers' unions can act like this (and they do), how much more tempting is it for teachers and schools who really DO have something to offer?

Another in-house area of pride that asserts itself is the tendency to tolerate empire-building. What's that? Since so much of what we're all doing is ground-breaking, the folks who got in there early and got their hands dirty are probably going to take a lot of ownership in the resulting growth and fruit. That is natural and can be good. It can also go sour if they start to view "their area" as their little kingdom! "We wouldn't have a drama program at all if it weren't for me!" (Few would actually talk like that, but it sure can be thought and adopted as an attitude.) Woe betide the poor administrator or other staff member who dares to offer suggestions for change, or worse, encroaches on their turf! Once again, hard work offered with great humility is the key to keeping empires from forming.

**Financial snares*—As the Word says, money is often the springboard to many kinds of evil, or just complicated situations. So financial woes are many and diverse: enrollment pressures (the old adage about the budget expanding along with revenue is very true), salary and benefits for staff you want to retain, temptations to accept state/fed money offers ... etc., and beat goes on. Better facilities will cost more in every aspect. Stay focused here, too. How you spend money should reflect your philosophical priorities, not favorite areas of out-spoken board members or, worse, heavy donors.

The positive side: Opportunities accompanying growth

Growth, when it comes through being steadfast to your vision, is certainly a blessing. But you can't rest there, hard decisions will need to be made for planning quality growth:

**To high school or not to high school*—Certainly there are many aspects to consider on this, but without hesitation, my advice is do it! How else, when else will you see the "Fruit" of the Trivium? Of course it will cost a lot of money, eventually. But you will probably start with a just a few kids, anyway. And, trust me on this, kids attract kids! I have heard from a number of schools who have asked whether they should continue into the high school grades with just a small number of students then in eighth grade. Some of these schools actually stated that they thought they should "wait until we have enough kids to justify the cost." Good grief! That reminds me of the French generals who, during our War for Independence, said they would join the fight against the British as soon as the Americans were winning. Mr. Franklin rightly pointed out to them that should that happen, the Americans wouldn't need them! In other words, you should grow with what you have, not what you hope to get. If you have families who are willing to stick with you, stick with them, by all means possible! Some students will have to be the pioneers, the trailblazers or, in a less romantic vein (as our first students called themselves) ... the guinea pigs. It may mean virtually tutoring them for a while, with costs being subsidized by the elementary fees. So be it. Lord willing, those younger students will significantly gain from the investment their parents put into the fledgling secondary, years before. And don't fall into the trap of thinking facilities are what make a solid secondary (e.g. well-equipped labs, large gym, arts, etc.). Repeat after me: It's the teachers and the philosophy, not the brick and mortar.

Trust me, all the sweat and concerns will have their validation time when your first class of seniors crosses the stage during your first graduation!

True-Life Dramas: The Turning Point for our Secondary...

By 1986-87, we knew we needed to resolve the matter of our hemorrhaging, so to speak, from the seventh and ninth grades. Putting it in less disgusting terms, we were losing kids to the "public" junior high and/or high school each year. We theorized long and hard about this problem, and determined that it seemed to come down to two major reasons: 1) We didn't have all the bells and whistles (sports, dances, cool stuff) that the public secondary programs did, and 2) Kids attract kids. Since we were losing more than we were gaining at that level, getting more to attract others was rather problematic. It also wasn't hard to rank those reasons in terms of need for action: if we didn't retain the kids, starting any other extracurricular programs would be a bit difficult.

Thus, in the spring of 1987, we were down to a total of about fourteen seventh and eighth graders, with no high schoolers at all. The elementary was doing fine, numbers wise, but it looked like those parents who wanted us to stop at eighth grade were going to get their wish, de facto. The board made this issue a top priority of planning and discussion. It was decided that we would hold a meeting with just the parents of our current eighth graders, five in all (down from twelve two years earlier). This would be an essentially do-or-die meeting. We were going to ask these parents to answer one, all-important question: "What would we have to do to, as a board, to persuade them to have their students graduate from Logos High School?" Considering that Logos High School was a theoretical program at the time, this was asking for a lot from these parents.

We met with the five sets of parents in Larry Lucas's home. After a bit of hemming and hawing we got down to The Question, and requested that they try not to let the others' answers influence their own. We needn't have worried. These families had already demonstrated their independent thinking just by having their students at Logos School for as long as they had. I will admit I was a bit on pins and needles. Very realistically, the future of Logos School's secondary program would be determined that night, by these parents. That was the thought that ran through my mind, causing me the same kind of sweaty anticipation political candidates must have on election night.

My fears dissipated and my stomach muscles relaxed in waves of relief, as each parent around the room gave essentially the same answer:

"Well, we aren't interested in sports or other programs that much. Otherwise we would have left sooner. We know Logos doesn't offer much in the way of nifty facilities, or fancy equipment. Basically, we put our kids in Logos to get the best, God-centered education we could find. Our bottom line for keeping our kids there is this: if you continue to hire and keep the kind of godly, loving teachers you have, we'll keep our kids in Logos until they graduate. That's the deal."

What a deal! It still implied a very serious responsibility on our part, but it was one we had embraced from the very beginning as an unchanging goal. We very happily accepted the terms of their deal. Later that spring, we made a big hoopla (promotion ceremony, cake, even letter jackets) celebrating these five students moving into our high school. Four years later, by God's sustaining grace, we had the joy of not only seeing those same five students receive their diplomas; we awarded six more to the students who had joined the class in the intervening years. This pioneering class and their parents, literally blazed the path to graduation that many other secondary students would follow.

Back to *other* Opportunities Accompanying Growth

**Vision-enhancing programs*—With growth and maturity, you want to deepen everyone's understanding and commitment to your vision. So...

- Bring in speakers to train staff, parents, students (we were blessed greatly to have Doug Wilson in-house, so to speak) at specially planned events. (Hint: If you want parents to come, include the kids in a program and/or have food!)
- Commission qualified staff to write specific materials to use at school and maybe sell.
- Plan more and larger communications to families e.g. book giveaways, in-school seminars, better brochures—all from

well-developed thinking about growth.

**Community reputation/influence*—Quality work, consistently done year after year, produces a hard-earned, but well-earned reputation; there will be portions of the community who are thrilled to see how you are fulfilling your mission because they love to see any kids getting a quality education. There will be other portions of the community (sadly, including some believers) who will consider you elitist, as well as uncaring about the government schools. But if God blesses you with consistently high standards and achievements, there will be other tangible blessings from the community, e.g. auction contributions from businesses that respect the school, free advertising in news stories (which you need to very carefully monitor), and you may even have the experience of families moving to your community, or just closer into town, primarily to put their kids in your school. The local Chamber of Commerce and the real estate agents will love you for that!

**Christian community benefits*—Trust, which must be earned over time, is an extremely valuable commodity. If your Christian community is somewhat typical, it is likely few of the local evangelical churches will leap to support you from the outset. But don't despair, it may be that they are trying to be cautious and are waiting to see if you fulfill your grand rhetoric. If you do, year after year, then you should start to see more families coming from a wider variety of churches (assuming that is okay with your admissions standards, which I hope it is!). Our existence and work as a non-denominational Christian school has, I believe, been a significant unifying element in our area, i.e. parents meeting parents from different churches, where otherwise their paths never would have crossed.

**Internal benefits*—These should become rather obvious, but still they are a joy to see, e.g. curriculum maturity, staff longevity, long-term parents as ambassadors attracting others, no need to advertise, maturing board, increasing trust between staff and admin, admin and board, easier to consider and plan for long-term, and even track graduates' lives.

**Sister school assistance*—Maturity, particularly in our unique brand of education, brings with it the real opportunity and accompanying responsibility to help other younger, or starting schools in your region. Sort of sowing of the seed, if you will. Or just sharing what you have learned. But there is a mutual benefit from inter-school visits between schools of a similar vision and philosophy: sharing of discoveries, practical wisdom, fellowship, and just encouragement to know you're no longer the only ones doing this!

Accreditation—There's a lot to be said about seeking and obtaining some form of outside accreditation. To keep it simple here, I would recommend you seek it from ACCS (Association of Classical, Christian Schools). There are obviously other options, but this was designed by and for classical, Christian educators. I wrote an article on the basic ideas behind accreditation a while back. I trust you will find it helpful.

STATE ACCREDITATION VS. EXCELLENCE IN EDUCATION

I considered entitling this column "State Accreditation—The Golden Cow of Education," but upon reflection felt that that would be unkind. Cows get enough bad press as it is.

It is rare, when I interview new families, that one of the parents does not ask about our accreditation status with the state. It is also very common that they inquire about the certification requirements we place upon our teaching applicants. Understandable questions, given the conditioning to which we, as a culture, have been subject. We have been told, both directly and subliminally, that state accreditation is to education what the FDA stamp of approval is to food quality, i.e. the guarantee of rigorous scrutiny by knowledgeable experts. The only problem is that if the FDA's stamp indicated the same "quality" in food that state accreditation does for schools, salmonella and hepatitis would be as common as the cold and we'd all resort to raising our own food. Not too surprisingly, many people have done just that in education; they've started their own schools!

The idea of holding educational institutions and their instructors accountable and ensuring they maintain high standards is very appropriate. However, at least two things need to be carefully considered:

WHO or WHAT is the superior and responsible agency to which the institution is accountable?

WHAT STANDARDS are used as the yardstick against which the institution is being measured?

It's very disappointing to me to see so many Christians become schizophrenic (Latin—"split mind") on this issue. On most other issues involving children and their training, most Christians resort immediately to the Scriptures. To cut to the chase, the Bible **clearly** and without apology says **parents** are the primary educators. They are the "WHO" to which any institution educating children must be accountable. The State has been given no biblical authority in education. Doesn't it then follow that the "STANDARDS" are also up to the parents, within certain, specified biblical principles?

If all this isn't convincing enough, consider two other points—has state accreditation (a relatively new idea on the block, historically) consistently bequeathed us better and better educated citizens, or just the opposite? Further, the actual accreditation process gives barely a nod to the academic performance of a school's students. Instead, it majors on the physical plant and faculty numbers.

At Logos we not only believe we operate directly under the collective authority of our families (as verbalized and channeled by our board), a large percentage of our staff is comprised of parents. The standards we hold all our staff members to, and the school at large, come from the Bible. Therefore, loving the children and modeling the Christian life to them are enforced standards. In the end, the excellence of any education is discerned by the quality evidenced in the lives of the students, not by state-approved, meaningless certificates.

(Just for your info, since this column was written, we have: 1. Earned and then declined ACSI accreditation, 2. Earned and kept accreditation from ACCS—the Association of Classical Christian Schools.)

Setting up for the future

Growth may indicate God wants you around for awhile. Without being presumptuous, you need to meet the needs of current and future families and staff members who are/will be committed to your school.

Planning is critical, even though we all understand plans will change—All our initial efforts at beginning a school are sort of like planning for a wedding: You almost suffocate in the details for that first day. Then it flies by and, just like a marriage, you discover you have a life together (with school families and staff) in front of you now. It is absolutely critical that you give some quality thought time to your purposes, goals, and long-term plans. After all, your little school just might end up affecting many students' lives, unto generations to come. Don't sweat getting all the plans just right—they will certainly change as the future becomes the present. Fine. Then you know what worked and what didn't, or maybe put another way, whether God blessed in the way you thought He would, or in a way that was better.

Hint: Find someone who knows how to walk your board through a formal process of *strategic planning*. This is a process of identifying your school's weaknesses, strengths, challenges, obstacles, etc. Then you formulate some ideas for meeting the challenges particularly. There's obviously a lot more to it, but you hopefully get the idea. It is kind of weird at the outset, but it can illustrate some critical issues your board should consider and plan for, if possible.

Philosophy/policies/practices—tough cases make bad laws, principled decisions, not expedient ones—Challenges will continue to come so, just as with your faith, walk in what you know to be right, not proceed on worldly wisdom or succumb to pressures to make expedient, bad calls. God honors His principles—blessings follow hard, but right calls. I have been asked repeatedly by young schools "When can we expect clear sailing?" They mean when will things smooth out for them. It's tempting at this point to get sarcastic and laugh derisively, but that's not helpful. Neither does it reflect the truth of reality. No, there is no "smooth sailing" point, but there are problems you grow past, thank God. Other problems, sometimes knottier ones come in, but that's how we learn and mature in God's grace.

Here's a column on some of the issues we've weighed and considered in light of what we believe we are to do:

Why don't we...?

*"All things are lawful, but not all things are **profitable**. All things are*

lawful, but not all things ***edify****. Let no one seek his own good, but that of his neighbor." -I Corinthians 10:23, 24*

Most of the time I like to fill this column with some allusion to those things we *do* as a classical, Christian school to fulfill our philosophical and biblical purposes. Sometimes I wrap a theme in an illustration, and other times I just lay out the raw case, so to speak, in the hope that it will help the collective "you," particularly our parents, understand and hopefully "amen" what is being done here. Since we are here for up to thirteen years for some of our students, it behooves us to give you reasons for your year-to-year support of, and involvement in, Logos. But not all of those reasons are necessarily things we *do*; there are lots of things we *don't* do as a result of our philosophical and biblical base. You should know those, as well.

Below, I have made a short list of topics that range from the lack-luster to the possibly volatile, but all share the common aspects of: 1) we *don't* do them and 2) we are frequently asked why we don't. I will try to be lucid, but each of these topics requires its own column, at least, so please understand I am going for *brevity* and clarity. So forgive my possibly not succeeding with the latter by attempting the former.

Why doesn't Logos...

Provide sex and drug awareness programs? We aren't prudes nor Victorian. We don't need to be: the lack of success by the plethora of the government-sponsored anti-drug, anti-baby programs should be as obvious as daylight to everyone. Why don't they work? These areas require long-term, *moral* grounding, not brain-power. Kids know sex can make babies and they know drugs can kill you. "So what's the big deal? They're both fun for a while, and that's the point of living, isn't it?" God and godly parents are *best* equipped to answer that life view question, not us.

Seek state accreditation? Children are made in the image of God, not Caesar (the State). We are under biblical parental authority, not the State's. At the risk of sounding anti-American to some ears, the government was not intended by God, or our founding fathers, to educate children. Again, the results speak for themselves. State accreditation is far from synonymous with quality education. Next question.

Celebrate Martin Luther King, Jr. Day? Among other reasons, we don't think the jury's been out long enough to put Dr. King on the same level as, say, George Washington Carver, for significant contributions to all men. Scripture takes the long view in weighing a man's works. Carver, and many others, have stood the test of time and biblical scrutiny by generations. We will honor him and those similarly proven.

Have computers for the students to use in the classrooms? We've been there, tried that (on a limited scale), and went back to doing what we do best—using teachers and books in the classrooms. Please don't misunderstand; we teachers and administrators like computers (I really like this newly donated one I am fingering now!), but they cost too much for us to provide; they're upgraded every other week; the kids learn them faster and have better ones at home; and we frankly just don't think they're as good for real education, as, say, books and teachers.

Do lots of various fundraisers? We've been there, too; from can drives, to candy sales, to selling chili dogs at a booth, to even Christmas tree sales. Out of consideration for our families and our reputation in the community, we earnestly try to limit the number of times and ways we stick out our corporate hand. Sure, we need all the help God directs our way. That means we don't want neighbors pestered by Logos students or parents freezing, frying or just plain bored by spending hours in booths or on the streets. For more on this, talk to Ed Van Nuland, our development director.

Use just "Christian" publishers for our materials? The answer to that is simply and politely, because they don't do the job we require. We have developed our own curriculum guides trying to implement a classical, Christian program, and no single, current publisher, Christian or secular, can provide us with all the right stuff. Currently we use over fifty publishers, but we have found that, in more and more situations, if we want a certain text, we must either find an original title (not a textbook), or we write the materials ourselves. We really don't mind; it's kind of fun.

Put on just "Christian" drama productions? Having just presented an extremely well-received, albeit secular high school play, this is the time of year we might hear this. The answer is very similar to the one above regarding "Christian" textbooks. When God commanded the Israelites to plunder the Egyptians' gold and gems, He set forth a principle for His people from that time forward. That is, nothing truly good *belongs* to the wicked; they can only borrow it for a while. It ultimately belongs to the children of light who will inherit the earth. In that regard then, "Christian" and "secular" lose their meaning. Quality, like beauty, justice, and truth, all bring glory to His Name, wherever found. Conversely, sad to say, in our age the "Christian" label attached to many items is often as inappropriate as "Honorable" attached to Member of Congress.

Have many discipline problems? The wrong answer to that is because we only accept "good" kids. There are no naturally "good" kids, anymore than there are naturally weed-less gardens. Well-behaved students, like the gardens of Versailles, have been painstakingly cared for and tended by those who love them. Spanking a naughty child, along with other forms of consistent, loving discipline, is like pulling weeds in that child's life. Students coming to us from parents with that mind-set will not be a problem for us in the classroom. Respect and regard for authority are ingrained givens for these students. With that foundation firmly laid in their lives, we at Logos can then get on with the business at hand, appealing to their minds and encouraging their hearts.

Unwavering biblical standards/vision for the board members, staff— How does an institution stay faithful? The complicated answer is: By having leaders who stay faithful, day by day, to the Lordship of Jesus Christ. And remember, it was He who said, "each day has enough troubles of its own." But He also said "Give us THIS day our daily bread." God's covenants are with people, not institutions, so keep a proper perspective. Loyalty to your school, your staff is not only okay, but to be desired. Nevertheless, don't ever confuse your loyalty and support with what really keeps your school going—God's daily grace, poured out over time. So boast in the Lord! Even though I know Logos and all schools will end, our WORK is eternal, if it's done in His will, to His glory.

Conclusion: I realize that the above material on growth doesn't get into specific recommendations for particular facilities or programs. That was not an oversight: I didn't want to get into those things because every situation is so different in what a school faces. I know of schools who were given fifteen acres or a ton of money in their second year of operation. Other schools (like ours) went for many years before we saw our first $10,000 gift. We had to build our facilities, once we had our own, out of a re-modeled roller skating rink. I am not complaining—it was wonderful to see the changes over time. I firmly believe we—everyone in the school—were much more grateful for each improvement than we would have been had we received everything all at once.

I purposely focused my counsel for future planning on what I consider the MOST important considerations, i.e. sticking to and promulgating your philosophy. Granted, building and buildings get people excited (especially the guys) and it's easy to spend a lot of time and energy at the board level discussing facilities. But that's why you need to be the one to remind everyone of the balance: yes, facilities matter, but frankly you can teach a class almost anywhere. Make the main purpose of the school the priority and all these things will be added unto you. All other planning should be an exciting outgrowth of the original and maintained vision.

CHAPTER ELEVEN

Review and Miscellaneous Stuff

The seventh law of teaching (John Milton Gregory) stresses the value and importance of review. I would be remiss as an administrator and a teacher if I assumed that you wouldn't benefit from a review. Therefore, in the brief statements below, I have summarized what I believe to be some of the key points from each chapter. (Did you notice that I cleverly put this summary at the end of the book so that you wouldn't cheat and jump right to this section without reading the longer version first? Administrators need to be sneaky sometimes, too.)

Chapter 1—Your Qualifications:

- The head administrator of the school is the face of the school. Make it a good face! Enjoy people, kids, greatly.
- You are responsible for everything that happens in the school—but don't panic.
- Have a plan for dealing with everything before it happens. Or, at least, be able to make one on the fly.

- Work hard, very hard, as unto the Lord Himself. Don't expect a parade in your honor or even frequent thank-yous, then you will be nicely surprised when they come.
- Stay right with God and man, as much as it depends on you. Particularly with your wife and kids.
- Remember you are the lighthouse keeper—guard and maintain the flame well.

Chapter 2—School Start-up: Planning for the Practicalities

- Know your philosophy so clearly that it comes through loud and clear in all your guidelines and practices, including your initial orientation and training of your teachers.
- Have a place for everything and a enforce a means to get everything back in its place.
- Anticipate and meet the basic needs for teacher materials. It's hard enough to teach—give them the tools they need.
- Ensure everyone knows their realm of responsibility and service, as well as who they go to for help and direction.

Chapter 3—Board Diplomacy

- Never underestimate the power of the board—for the good or ill of the school. It has only two gears—forward or reverse.
- There are well-known, but too little practiced, effective principles by which the board should conduct its business.
- In an ideal world your board would have no problems with having an all-male board. Whatever your situation, the biblical home must be represented appropriately in your school, from the board down.
- The board members must understand and be committed to the corporate, vs. individual, nature of the board.
- Most importantly, the board must lead the school spiritually by how its members conduct themselves particularly when meeting.

Chapter 4—Staff Considerations

Hiring

- The best way to get the people you want is to know what you're looking for. Have clear standards and stick to them.
- Hands down, parents are your best bet for great staff members. They have the understanding and commitment you want from your staff. Competence can be somewhat determined by looking at their kids.
- Use a variety of counselors (you and the board or committee) to carefully screen each applicant.
- Evaluations are absolutely necessary even if they make teachers uncomfortable. They need the good feedback.

Men and Women Are Different

- Ignore popular or politically correct views and stick with biblical standards regarding men and women.
- Study the differences and use them wisely in making assignments in the school.
- Tailor your communications, with the differences in mind, to everyone's benefit.
- Never settle for an unhealthy spiritual climate among your staff. Righteousness is not an option—it's a necessity.

Volunteers

- Include as many as possible, but don't put them in critical positions. Be willing to pay for what you really need done.

Chapter 5—Families

Admissions/Gate-keeping: Believers & Non-believers

- You need to be part, a key part, of determining which students enter your school.
- Your board should know what their philosophy of accepting students is: Reform school, open enrollment, or "covenantal." (The last one is the right one—building on a biblical training model, even for non-believers.

- Have a well-structured way of bringing a new family into the school and becoming clearer on what you are all about.

Parents

- Families come with varying levels of understandings and, therefore, commitment levels to your school's philosophy of education. Classical education takes a lot of explaining.
- Interviews should include both parents, if at all possible. In any case, they should agree that this is where they want their children.
- Don't take or keep a child whose parents will not or can not control him. Don't try to be a parent, in other words, even if you know better than they do.

Kids—boys/girls

- The world will try to tell you that differences, if they exist, don't matter in school. Even some Christians have bought that hogwash. Study the children and the Word. You'll figure it out.
- Use the different traits that you see to your advantage in teaching and guiding in a Christian, classical context.
- Emphasize their roles in encouraging and requiring good manners. Yes, even and especially at the upper grades.
- Don't you dare try to be their primary or even best source for spiritual training. We are NOT their parents or the Church.

Chapter 6—Discipline/rules/standards

- Adopt a clear, biblically just and comprehensive policy. Promulgate it. Do it. All the time. Really.
- Establish guidelines that make it clear what the teachers should do in most situations. Do that, too.
- Remember the goal of discipline—a cheerful, God-controlled person, and train to that.

Chapter 7—Curriculum planning/development/materials

- Surprise! Your curriculum needs to be so obviously linked to your classical philosophy that you should be able to draw an imaginary straight line from what and how you teach, anywhere in your school, to a tenet in your philosophy statement. (You wouldn't believe how many Christian schools would find that a news item!)
- A curriculum guide must be present, practical, comprehensive, and constantly reviewed for improvement.
- Your materials should be carefully chosen; don't buy the complete offerings of any publisher, even us. Nobody fits your school's needs and purposes that well! Chose the best and if you can't find it, make it.
- But the most important, the absolutely biggest "E" on your school's classical, curricular success is how your teachers teach! Don't let them teach the way they were taught, unless they went to the only school in the U.S. at that time that taught the Trivium and the tools of learning.
- You will all need to study the most effective, consistent methods that match the kids' levels and still challenge them appropriately.

Chapter 8—Daily Management/ Programs/Scheduling

Facility issues

- Managing means daily work—for you. You'd better enjoy ensuring there's "a place for everything," than ensuring that everything regularly goes back into its place. (Not all done by you: clear assignments and delegation, my son. That's the ticket.)
- Do you see what I see?" It's not just a Christmas tune; it's the message your janitorial staff should get. That is, if *you* can see "it" (garbage in the hall corners, dirty sinks, etc.), then they can, too, and they should deal with it.
- Insist on security measures being in place at night. Practice

common sense safety during the day and leave the rest to God's care for your kids and school.

Financial issues

- If your tuitions don't cover all the expenses, then remember the 80/20 rule (tuitions shouldn't bring in less than about 80% of revenue, gifts shouldn't exceed 20%).
- Pay your teachers and staff as much as possible, then pay them more next year. Find benefits that your school can afford and offer them as soon as possible. You won't spend money on a better investment for your school than your staff members.
- Consider creative ideas as needed: lower tuitions at the lower levels to encourage folks to come in. Possibly "freeze" tuitions for long-time families to give them a break.
- Pay your bills on time, especially locally. It engenders good will, not a bad thing to have coming your way.
- Make sure you have internal controls that keep even the appearances respectable.
- Include your staff in developing your annual budget, then insist on a balanced one.
- This may be part of basic economics, but it helped me (not having HAD basic economics): make sure you have a "pigeon hole" for every possible expenditure. And there will be LOTS of them.

Programs/Scheduling

- Okay, pop question (you'd better get this one by now!): What should drive your selection and practices of holidays, days of remembrance, vacations, etc.? Hmmm? If you immediately thought, "Our philosophy!," you win! Give yourself some chocolate. (If you didn't think of that, well, you figure out some appropriate self-punishment.)
- Keep examining what you celebrate and how. Over the years

you may want to drop some things and add others, but the process should reflect a growing maturity, not whims.

- Consider the practical side of things in your planning, too. Your staff, facilities, amount of time out of class, etc., should all be weighed in the balance.
- Obviously, biblically-based events pull rank on anything else. Even these, however, need some serious, philosophically-driven thought in how you practice/honor the event.
- Scheduling your days, quarters, semesters, and years should enable you to get the most bang for the parents' bucks possible. The schedules should therefore give your teachers the best amount of time, within reason and balance, remembering that the kids have families, too.

Chapter 9—Development/Community relations

- If you think you can't afford a development officer, think again. Do you LIKE being the development officer/PR guy, as well as the administrator? Somebody's got to do it, why not get someone you can train (i.e. get trained) to do it right?
- A good development person is an excellent investment for the school. Not only does he foster good will for your school now, and bring in some needed buckaroos, he lays plans for the future support of your school.
- You want a humble, yet forthright person who can ask for money, yet obviously care personally about the donor.
- Start him with the goal of at least getting the equivalent of his salary in gifts the first year, then slowly increase target goals. Pay him a decent salary, by the way. Don't pay him in any kind of percentage of gifts obtained—bad form, old man. Tacky and frowned on, even by the secularists.

Chapter 10—Growth

- Expect growth in quantity, but only if your school is growing in quality. Plan for it.

- Rose-colored glasses, like your brief honeymoon period, don't change the way people are. Don't get discouraged, but be realistic. You will have people come and go for all sorts of reasons, dumb and otherwise. Stick to your course.
- The longer your school exists and the larger it gets, the bigger the target it will become for the opposition. Here again, expect it and know the positive things you need to do, as well as what to avoid. Mission drift is one name for a deadly disease your school can and will suffer, if you are not faithful to the Scriptures and/or your philosophy.
- Grow into a full-orbed trivium. Get that high school going ASAP.
- You won't be there forever, so design and record your labors such that your work is a well-shaped baton to pass on to the next guy. (That's one big reason I'm doing the tons of work this handbook has taken!)
- Help your board frequently and regularly (annual planning) look beyond the present and lift their eyes to the future. What is their vision for five, ten, twenty years? Think long-term. You have a school, remember? You're not designing a boutique. Build for the next generation, at all times.

THE BATTLE OF IDEAS AND IDOLS—CHANGES, CHALLENGES, CONTROVERSIES, INEVITABLE CONFLICT

I thought I would throw in a number of seemingly unrelated issues and ideas that have come our way. The common element is that they all faced us and we had to deal with them in some manner.

Colliding with ADD, ADHD, ETC. AD INFINITUM...

It's not a matter of if, but when, you will have to face this recent but lasting phenomenon. I certainly don't claim to be an expert on all that has been churned out about learning disabilities, but I have had some experience with teaching children. Let's just say, the brain is a marvelous and mysterious tool that God made. We don't have all the answers to its machinations. But we DO know Who made it, as well as what He said about teaching kids. I submit the following, therefore, for your consideration.

Who's got the RIGHT diagnosis? ADD, ADHD, ODD, LIES

"They interrupt ... they don't follow directions. In short, they do what seizes them at the moment without thinking through the consequences."

"Accept the fact that it is a handicap ... don't expect your child to behave like others." (Sandra Doran, on children with "ADHD"; *Focus On the Family*)

"Even a child is known by his deeds, whether they are pure and right."

"Children, be obedient to your parents in all things, for this is well-pleasing to the Lord." (**God**, on children with sin natures; the Bible, Prov. 20:11, Col. 3:20)

History of "Disabilities"

Personal experience:

When I was doing my student teaching at Moscow High School a "few" years ago, as part of my experience I was assigned to regularly teach art to a group of handicapped students. I grew very fond of these students and we had an all too short time together. We were able to complete the painting of a pretty nifty wall-mural, though. Among these students were kids in wheelchairs, kids with Down's Syndrome, and others with a variety of mental and physical problems. However, they had at least a couple of things in common; one was they all had medically provable disabilities, the second was that they all had a generally cheerful and compliant spirit. I had few discipline problems with them, after the class rules were made clear.

General history—handicaps were medically identifiable, treated as such, then mainstreaming, growing demand for "equal education" coupled with increasingly poor education = Learning Disabilities growth of special ed, follow the money!

In the years since the days of real handicaps there has been a flood of previously undetected "disabilities" diagnosed. It reminds one of FDR's "alphabet soup" of programs to fix the economy during the Depression. Considering his legacy, the comparison is not a bad fit.

Definitions: LD, ADD, ADHD, and my favorite, a relatively new release, ODD, Oppositional Defiant Disorder. Quotes from advertisement for workshop: "Symptoms—Lose their temper? Argue with adults? Deliberately do things that annoy others? Blame others for their own mistakes? Are touchy or easily annoyed by others? But ODD students are not merely misbehaving, difficult young people. They are often sensitive, intelligent, capable students who need someone to help unlock their potentials." "Workshops? Diagnosis and medical management of ODD students. The underlying and sometimes unseen causes of ODD. Attitudinal Therapy techniques."

The symptoms for these afflictions read as specifically as your daily horoscope: "Your fellow workers need your timely input today." "Today holds many challenges for you, do your best in decision making and your future will be bright." "To avoid explosive situations, don't smoke around gas pumps." What kind of diagnoses are these? Just about every kid and virtually every adult male I know could be labeled ADD, if not ADHD, but most certainly ODD at some time or other. The next one I trust we'll see is the unabashed—LIES—Learning Isn't Essential Syndrome, which already afflicts millions of students as well as teachers. The truly ironic aspect to this is that all these recently revealed "handicaps" are being brought to us by the same establishment that has produced over twenty million functionally illiterate adults in the last twenty-five years. Doesn't it strike you as odd that we are able to simultaneously produce the most poorly educated generation in our country's history and yet "discover" all these subtle, mysterious learning and behavioral problems that previous generations failed to notice? How can we know so much about children's brains and their learning capabilities and yet have a lower proportion of reading adults than 100 years ago? Not to mention behavioral problems that would cause the hair of any prior generation of teachers to turn white!

Treatment (as in illness) vs. Solution (as in problem) options

In one sense, this epidemic of pathetic diagnoses is predictable and understandable. It is hard to see children struggle with a problem. Education in this country has, particularly in the last 130 years, caused a great deal of suffering of children. When one of our children is having problems, whether it is difficulty learning the multiplication tables or a cough that won't go away, as loving parents we will seek a way to help this little one. What parent or teacher can sit by and calmly watch a child suffer? But before we act, doesn't it make sense to try to diagnose the real problem? We don't put a band-aid on a child's sore throat or give them Tums for a scraped knee. So, if it is an illness or medical problem we look for medical solutions, not solutions as in dealing with a correctable problem such as misbehavior. Today, all sorts of "experts" will tell us what is best for our children, especially when it comes educating them. Doesn't it make sense to listen to someone who has not only vast experience, but successful experience with solving problems like the ones we see? Who would take their child to a doctor whose success rate was less than 50%? Yet vast numbers of parents, even Christian parents, seek advice on raising and educating children from "professionals" who have an even worse rate of true accomplishment. One of the most distressing interviews I heard on tape was a panel discussion conducted by no less an honorable man than Dr. James Dobson on the issue of ADD. Parents and experts swapped sad tales of ADD's inevitable affect on their children. What to do? And over and over the lament—"We did all we could to be good parents." What about seeking out non-"professional", but very successful godly parents and grandparents for advice that has meat in it. So how is it to be treated? What prescription is offered? Obviously, discipline is to be withheld, in direct contradiction to biblical admonitions for addressing bad behavior. You don't punish a child for having a cold, why would you punish them (or their parents) for a mental or personality syndrome? This trend really shouldn't be that surprising since we live in a culture that is actively seeking new names and causes for old sins. Drunkenness, homosexuality, even spewing foul-language has now been "linked" to genetics. God calls them sin; the world calls them syndromes.

One pandemic-wide, money-making, answer then—drug them into submission. What began thirty years ago as concern for just the students' problems with understanding lessons has descended to encouraging drug abuse in a last ditch effort to control behavior! The drug of choice is the increasingly popular Ritalin, an amphetamine. One doctor has written a book, a big one, calling for an anti-drug campaign in treating these LDs: (Quotes from *Talking Back to Ritalin* by Dr. Peter Breggin)

"Ritalin is a form of speed."

"The US Drug Enforcement Administration has issued a warning that Ritalin is highly addictive and a common drug of abuse comparable to amphetamine and cocaine."

"There is no convincing evidence that children with ADHD have anything physically wrong with them."

"The attention deficit is not in the child, but in us as adults. We need to find new and better ways to meet the child's needs, and we must find the will and time to do so. In modern America, there is little incentive to spend time with children and a great deal of incentive to spend time at other activities, including 'making a living.'"

Loving vs. Hating Children

A. God is not silent on educating children. Before we accept child-training advice, much less drugs, from a God-hating, child-killing culture, shouldn't we at least examine God's Word? What are some of His principles for educating all children? They include: loving, patient discipline, nourishment within order, punishment of disobedient behavior, patience with the weak, constant repetition of necessary instruction, modeling in all things, allowing maturity to take its course—not circumventing it or forcing it, giving them what they NEED, not what they always want—taking the long view of education—"when he is old..." (Prov. 22:6).

God loves our children even more than we do; wouldn't it make sense to consistently, not sporadically, trust and practice His methods? We in the late twentieth century, for all our technology and degrees, have not discovered fundamental things about training our children that our blessed Father forgot or neglected to tell us in His Word.

No, the Bible does not tell us directly how to help a child struggling with math, but it does directly tell us why children misbehave the way they often do. It also clearly tells us parents what to do for our children.

When consistently heeded, God's diagnosis and prescriptions will never fail to produce lasting benefits for our precious children. He promised.

MATTHEW 18 APPLIES EVEN IN SCHOOL

"And if your brother sins, go and reprove him **in private***; if he listens to you, you have won your brother. But if he does not listen to you, take one or two more with you, so that by the mouth of two or three witnesses every fact may be confirmed." -Matthew 18:15, 16*

There. It had happened again. Though hopefully unnoticeable to the person on the other side of my desk, my knee had definitely jerked. Worse, my knuckles were whitening—surely I couldn't hide that. Breathe deeply, relax those muscles. Now, focus on what she is saying.

"...and after talking to all those other moms, I found that I'm really not the only parent in the class who feels this way about Mrs. Burkstock's science test last week. In fact, after I told them my concerns, several of them said they felt exactly the same way, but were not sure if they should say anything to her. I mean, nobody wants to hurt her feelings, you know what I mean?"

Yes, I knew what she meant. With the kindest of intentions, what she really meant was that gossiping is a whole lot easier and less awkward than individually confronting a teacher with her concerns. Gossip? Surely that is a bit harsh, isn't it? "He who goes about as a slanderer reveals secrets, therefore do not associate with a gossip" (Prov. 20:19). But surely there was no slander intended; she only wanted to see if others "felt the same way." And what "way" was that? Eliminating all the hyperbole, these parents believed the teacher had made a poor call, a significant lapse in judgment, in giving the test.

So, what's wrong with a few parents comparing "notes" about a teacher's (or administrator's or board's) actions, without consulting her? Don't they have the right to do that? After all, the teacher is teaching *their* children. A number of years ago I was asked to go to another Christian school to "trouble-shoot" and give them some advice. Oh boy. After arriving at the school, it took me all of half-a-day to ascertain two facts: 1) this school had the worst problems I had ever personally seen, and 2) that a great portion of those problems stemmed from parents, staff, and board members all "just talking" to each other; they just hadn't bothered to confront the *right* people (i.e. those that could do something) about the problems. It had been far easier and more gratifying to talk behind each other's backs. Among other suggestions, I urged their board to adopt the principle of Matthew 18 in their school.

Certainly in Matthew 18 our Lord is directly addressing a suspected sin, vs. bad judgment calls, but as with many portions of Scripture certain principles can be derived from the direct teaching. Gossip or slander is addressed frequently in the Bible, from Proverbs to James. (James devotes all of chapter 3 to just what damage the tongue can do!) If the purpose of our Lord's directives in Matthew 18 was *not* to avoid groundless rumors and slander, what is the point of going to the person privately? By going first to the person under suspicion, gossip (a real sin) is avoided. Besides, by going first to the correct person, both sides of an issue are then heard, and it often turns out that at least part of the concern was based on inaccurate information. (For example, kids don't always give all sides of a story.)

I have seen far more damage than good done, even when a specific "sin" was not the initial problem, by people discussing the concern with everyone except the person who could do something positive. As one of our own "prophets," Bob Dylan, has said, "If you're not part of the solution, you're part of the problem." Christian school staff members, like most folks, are susceptible to the hurt that comes from discovering others have been talking behind their backs. Almost always an immediate feeling of betrayal of trust and friendship results. (At the school mentioned above, peace was not restored before almost the entire staff had been fired or resigned.)

On the other hand, many parents feel they should apologize when they do bring a concern directly to me or a teacher. They feel that they may be regarded as "complaining" or being a nuisance. Nothing could be further from the truth; by coming directly to the "source," they have done the right thing and avoided complaining to others, which is a real nuisance. Confrontations are about as fun as a trip to the dentist, but usually they are just as necessary. They can also be even more productive for all involved.

When a common spirit of trust and application of the *principle* in Matthew 18 exists in a Christian school setting, rumors and gossip rarely get a toehold. When the opposite happens, that is parents and teachers slandering others in the name of "concern," even Christian schools can be destroyed. It has happened and happened too often. The enemy of our souls frequently works to poison a Christian institution from the inside out, not from the outside in. Our Lord's wisdom still works well today, because He is in authority over all our schools and private lives.

That seems as good and appropriate a point as any to end this volume on. May the God and Father of our Lord Jesus Christ greatly bless and keep you and your school!

Soli Deo Gloria!

APPENDICES

Suggested Book List

As I mentioned earlier in this book, these are some titles I found helpful, for a variety of reasons, some even having to do with the details of administrating a school. But more having to do with WHY we are doing all this anyway. I recommend them to you as a short list of what I hope will become a much longer list of books you actually read. There are a growing number of folks starting to educate well, as well as a rich legacy of folks who did it well in the past—we should all read what these people have written.

The Abolition of Man by C.S .Lewis, Collier Books

Administration of the Christian School, edited by Roy W .Lowrie, Jr, ACSI

America's Christian History by Gary DeMar, American Vision

The Biblical View of Self-Esteem by Jay E. Adams, Harvest House Publishers

Call of Duty, The Sterling Nobility of Robert E. Lee, by J. Steven Wilkins, Highland Books

Carry a Big Stick, The Uncommon Heroism of Theodore Roosevelt by George Grant, Highland Books

The Case for Classical, Christian Education by Douglas Wilson, Canon Press

The Christian Philosophy of Education Explained by Stephen C .Perks, Avant Books

The Return of Dear Parents, A Collection of Newsletter Columns, by Tom Garfield, Logos School Materials

Excused Absence by Douglas Wilson, Crux Press
From Forgiven to Forgiving by Jay E. Adams, Calvary Press Publishing
A History of Christian School Education by ACSI
The Pattern of God's Truth by Frank E. Gaebelein, BMH Books
The Philosophy of the Christian Curriculum by R.J. Rushdoony, Ross House Books
Postmodern Times by Gene Edward Veith, Jr., Crossway Books
Recovering the Lost Tools of Learning by Douglas Wilson, Crossway Books
Repairing the Ruins, edited by Douglas Wilson, Canon Press
On Secular Education (booklet) by R.L .Dabney, Ransom Press
The Seven Laws of Teaching (original edition) by John M .Gregory, Veritas Press

Sample Documents:

Here are just a few samples that were referred to specifically in this manual. For a much larger collection I would encourage you to contact Logos Press.

LOGOS SCHOOL QUESTIONNAIRE FOR TEACHER INTERVIEWS

PURPOSE: To be used as a source for questions to ask prospective teachers during the administration's and board's interviews. Check off the questions used by indicating whether the question was answered satisfactorily or not. After completing the interview, please refer to the summary for making any comments.

APPLICANT'S NAME ______________________
*DATE OF INTERVIEW*________/_______/______
POSITION DESIRED __________________
*INTERVIEWER*______

GENERAL QUESTIONS:

SAT UNSAT

1. *Please state your understanding of the Gospel.*
2. *Please describe how and when you became a Christian.*
3. *Do you understand Logos School's basic doctrinal stance and Secondary Doctrine*

policy and do you agree with it? (Please give some examples of both primary and secondary doctrines.)

4. How does your spouse (parents, if unmarried) feel about your possibly assuming a position at a Christian school?

5. What is the spiritual condition (saved, unsaved) of your immediate family?

6. What church do you attend and how are you involved in it?

7. What is the basic cause when a Christian is not joyful?

8. What do believe is unique about Christian education?

9. Why do you want to teach in a Christian school?

10. Please give three characteristics of an outstanding teacher.

11. How do/would you incorporate those characteristics in your teaching?

12. How do you believe Creation should be taught?

13. What long-range plans/goals do you have?

14. Are you aware of the salary being offered for this position? If so, do you anticipate any hardship if you were to try to live with this level of income?

15. In addition to teaching, what other duties/responsibilities would you expect to have at Logos?

16. If you have taught before, please describe one of the worst experiences you had and one of the best and how you dealt with each.

17. What are the basic elements of good written communications?

18. Do you regularly apply these in your writing? What do you need to frequently work on?

19. From past work experiences, not teaching, please describe one accomplishment you had to work for and how you went about obtaining it.

20. Similarly, please describe one of the toughest jobs you had to do and why it was difficult for you.

21. How would past fellow employees describe you and your relations with them?

22. What personality characteristics do you have the hardest time relating to? How do you deal with them?

23. What types of leadership experiences have you had, and how did you go about organizing your group's tasks?

24. In your working style, do you prefer to plan extensively or do you work better spontaneously and intuitively?

25. Would your style have to change for this position? How?

26. What is your understanding of the authority/role of the Family, Church, State, and yours as a citizen?

SPECIFIC ,TASK-RELATED QUESTIONS:

1. *Why do you want to teach this particular class/subject?*
2. *What specific skills/training do you have that you believe will be the most beneficial to the students you would teach?*
3. *Dscribe your discipline standards and enforcement practices. (What is tolerable, what is not, how to plan for a minimum of class disruptions.)*
4. *How would you engage the students' minds through your teaching techniques for this class/subject?*
5. *What age-related characteristics would you expect to observe in this class/age of students?*
6. *Based on your understanding of The Lost Tools of Learning, what teaching methods/strategies would be most effective with this age group?*
7. *What does the integration of subject matter mean to you? Is it important/necessary?*
8. *If you believe integration of subjects is important, what are some ways you would practice this in your class(es)?*
9. *How would you express the Gospel to the students you would teach, considering their age-level?*
10. *How will you express a consistent, understandable, biblical worldview in your class(es)?*
11. *How much out-of-school time would you expect to put into preparing for your class(es)? (Hours per week)*
12. *In what ways, if any, would you try to incorporate parental help and input into your class(es)?*
13. *How important is communication with the parents? How would you normally communicate with the parents of your students?*
14. *In your opinion, what are the three most important things you can/should do for your students?*
15. *Describe some of your past students.*

LOGOS SCHOOL ELEMENTARY PRINCIPAL'S JOB DESCRIPTION AND ANNUAL EVALUATION FORM

Year________

Employee_:____

Key for Grading:

P = *Proficient,* **S** = *Satisfactory,* **U** = *Unsatisfactory,* **N/O** = *Not Observed*

Logos School expects employees to seek excellence. Unsatisfactory ratings require plans for steps toward correction and possible documented evidence indicating immediate concern.

Objectives	Grade	Comments
1. ORGANIZATION/MANAGEMENT		
Supervises the day-to-day operations of the kindergarten -sixth grades (referred to hereafter as the elementary)		
Monitors the needs of the elementary program and solves problems promptly		
Organizes various programs for the elementary (see required programs within the Elementary Yearly Programs)		
Schedules elementary school calendar		
Supervises ordering of general supplies, textbooks, and equipment for the elementary program		
2. FINANCE		
Follows purchasing policies when ordering elementary materials in order to remain within the budgeted amounts		
Ensures accurate records are maintained of all orders and expenses related to the elementary		
Secures procedures for safeguarding all cash and checks received for elementary programs		
3. DEVELOPMENT		
When appropriate, assists the Development Officer in elementary-related development projects and functions. The elementary principal will determine the occasion,frequency, and extent of any development assistance.		
4. RELATIONSHIP TO THE SUPERINTENDENT AND BOARD		
Defers to the superintendent in all matters of policy, work, and authority		

Supports board policy and decisions		
Keeps the superintendent informed of relevant issues affecting the elementary		
Keeps the superintendent informed of relevant issues affecting the elementary		
Effective in recruiting and preliminary interviewing of potential elementary staff members		
Acts as liaison between the elementary staff and the superintendent		
Ad Hoc member on various board subcommittees, as approved by the superintendent		
Follows the philosophy and goals of Logos School		
5. PARENT CONSTITUENCY		
Keeps parents informed of all relevant issues affecting the elementary		
Encourages active participation of parents in academic and other classroom elementary programs		
Submits written information regarding the elementary to the school's monthly newsletter		
Responds to and initiates regular and specific correspondence with parents and patrons		
Represents the elementary school to the public		
Is available to meet with parents and others		
6. INSTRUCTIONAL LEADERSHIP		
Keeps informed about all instructional aspects of the elementary (grammar) program		
Studies areas for curriculum improvement		
Encourages the growth of the elementary faculty through training, class visitations, workshops, etc.		
Conducts frequent elementary faculty meetings		
Oversees and enforces the elementary discipline program		
Organizes the administration of standardized testing to the elementary students		
Maintains and communicates his vision for classical and Christ-centered education to staff and students		
7. FACULTY-STAFF RELATIONS		
Organizes and executes a plan for elementary staff evaluation, improvements, makes recommendations to the superintendent regarding annual job assignments		
Delegates responsibility as appropriate		
Keeps his staff informed of all pertinent policies and information		

Is alert to staff morale level and seeks to be encouraging to his staff, and other employees		
Contacts, arranges for placement of aides, substitutes, and other necessary volunteer teachers		
Recommends/advises elementary staff retentions, dismissals to superintendent		
8. SPIRITUAL LEADERSHIP		
Displays leadership in spiritual growth		
Plans and coordinates elementary assemblies		
Monitors the overall spiritual maturity displayed by the elementary students and staff		
9. PROFESSIONAL AND PERSONAL		
Maintains and builds personal and professional development		
Maintains and displays high standards of personal ethics		
Represents the school with appropriate decorum		
Sets professional example for his staff		
10. MARKETING/PUBLIC RELATIONS		
Cooperates with the Marketing Officer and contributes ideas for materials production		
Seeks to upgrade the public image of the school and the elementary program		
Conducts elementary parent and student interviews		
Proposes policies for recruitment, application procedures, and admission standards for elementary students		
Maintains proper relationships and necessary communications with local churches		
Communicates as needed with other Christian and public schools and local businesses		
11. FACILITY MANAGEMENT		
Enforces and communicates high neatness and cleanliness standards within the elementary classrooms		
Suggests capital, and other improvements to the superintendent		
Assigns elementary classroom allocations		
Supports and assists in the overall facility maintenance/use standards for the entire facility		

****

OBJECTIVES FOR NEXT EVALUATION: Based on observations and annual board evaluation

SUMMARY:

EVALUATION SUMMARY:

Overall score:

AUTHENTICATION OF EVALUATION: The undersigned agree that this foregoing evaluation has been discussed between both parties:

Employee's signature: ______________________________
Date: ______________________________

Employer's signature: ______________________________
Date: ______________________________

LOGOS SCHOOL SECONDARY PRINCIPAL'S JOB DESCRIPTION AND ANNUAL EVALUATION FORM

*Year*_________

*Employee_:*____

Key for Grading:

P = *Proficient,* **S** = *Satisfactory,* **U** = *Unsatisfactory,* **N/O** = *Not Observed*

Logos School expects employees to seek excellence. Unsatisfactory ratings require plans for steps toward correction and possible documented evidence indicating immediate concern.

Objectives	**Grade**	**Comments**
1. ORGANIZATION/MANAGEMENT		
Supervises the day-to-day operations of the junior and senior high school (referred to hereafter as the secondary)		
Monitors the needs of the secondary program and solves problems promptly		
Organizes various programs for the secondary (see required programs within the Secondary Yearly Programs)		
Schedules secondary school calendar		
Supervises ordering of general supplies, textbooks, and equipment for the secondary program		

2. FINANCE		
Follows purchasing policies when ordering secondary materials in order to remain within the budgeted amounts		
Oversees the collection of specific secondary fees		
Ensures accurate records are maintained of all orders and expenses related to the secondary		
Secures procedures for safeguarding all cash and checks received for secondary programs		
3. DEVELOPMENT		
When appropriate, assists the Development Officer in secondary-related development projects and functions. The secondary principal will determine the occasion, frequency, and extent of any development assistance.		
4. RELATIONSHIP TO THE SUPERINTENDENT AND BOARD		
Defers to the superintendent in all matters of policy, work, and authority		
Supports board policy and decisions		
Keeps the superintendent informed of relevant issues affecting the secondary		
Effective in recruiting and preliminary interviewing of potential secondary staff members		
Acts as liaison between the secondary staff and the superintendent		
Ad Hoc member on various board subcommittees, as approved by the superintendent		
Follows the philosophy and goals of Logos School		
5. PARENT CONSTITUENCY		
Keeps parents informed of all relevant issues affecting the secondary		
Encourages active participation of parents in academic and extracurricular secondary programs		
Submits written information regarding the secondary to the school's monthly newsletter		
Responds to and initiates regular and specific correspondence with parents and patrons		
Represents the secondary school to the public		
Is available to meet with parents and others		
6. INSTRUCTIONAL LEADERSHIP		
Keeps informed about all instructional aspects of the secondary program		
Studies areas for curriculum improvement		

Encourages the growth of the secondary faculty through training, class visitations, workshops, etc.		
Conducts beneficial secondary faculty meetings		
Oversees and enforces the secondary discipline program		
Organizes the administration of standardized testing to the secondary students		
Ensures high school students have access to information regarding college entrance and provides and/or delegates assistance in completing admission applications and testing, e.g. the PSAT, ACT, and SAT		
Maintains and communicates his vision for classical and Christ-centered education to staff and students		
7. FACULTY-STAFF RELATIONS		
Organizes and executes a plan for secondary staff evaluation, improvements, makes recommendations to the superintendent regarding annual job assignments		
Delegates responsibility as appropriate (e.g. to AD)		
Keeps his staff informed of all pertinent policies and information		
Is alert to staff morale level and seeks to be encouraging to his staff, and other employees		
Recommends/advises secondary staff retentions, dismissals to superintendent		
8. SPIRITUAL LEADERSHIP		
Displays leadership in spiritual growth		
Plans and coordinates secondary assemblies		
Monitors the overall spiritual maturity displayed by the secondary students and staff		
9. PROFESSIONAL AND PERSONAL		
Maintains and builds personal and professional development		
Maintains and displays high standards of personal ethics		
Represents the school with appropriate decorum		
Sets professional example for his staff		
10. MARKETING/PUBLIC RELATIONS		
Seeks to upgrade the public image of the school and the secondary program		
Conducts secondary parent and student interviews/ Proposes guidelines for recruitment, application procedures, and admission standards for secondary students		
Maintains proper relationships and necessary communications with local churches		

Communicates as needed with other Christian and public schools, local businesses, and higher education institutions		
II. FACILITY MANAGEMENT		
Enforces and communicates high neatness and cleanliness standards within the secondary classrooms		
Suggests capital, and other improvements to the superintendent		
Makes effective secondary classroom allocations		
Supports and assists in the overall facility maintenance/use standards for the entire facility		

****

OBJECTIVES FOR NEXT EVALUATION: Based on observations and annual board evaluation

SUMMARY:

EVALUATION SUMMARY:

Overall score:

AUTHENTICATION OF EVALUATION: The undersigned agree that this foregoing evaluation has been discussed between both parties:

Employee's signature: ______________________________
Date: ______________________________

Employer's signature: ______________________________
Date: ______________________________

LOGOS SCHOOL DEVELOPMENT OFFICER EVALUATION FORM

YEAR:

Name:
Date of Evaluation:

KEY:
O = OUTSTANDING, S = SATISFACTORY, N = NEEDS WORK, U/O = UNOBSERVED DURING YEAR

OBJECTIVES	MARK	COMMENTS
A. FINANCIAL SUPPORT/FUNDRAISING:		
1. Increasing giving and meeting target amount for operational needs given year.		
2. Low cost-to-benefit ratio in work.		

3. Oversee and coordinate all school-wide fundraising efforts, especially auction.		
4. Raise, track needed month-to-month support in general and designated giving.		
5. Keeps superintendent informed of general giving amounts, compared to budget.		
6. Assist in coordination of long-term financial goals of the school.		
7. Seek to obtain grants from worthwhile foundations or individuals.		
B. PERSONAL/PUBLIC RELATIONS		
1. Respond to all donated gifts within 24 hours of receipt of gift.		
2. Become a visible participant in the community and spokesman for Logos School to civic, church, and business people.		
3. Assist superintendent in furthering relations with area pastors.		
4. Establish and build personal relationships with current and potential donors to the school.		
5. Seek to broaden support of the school through relationships with local businessmen.		
6. Plan informative events for specific groups to learn more about the school.		
C. COMMUNICATIONS		
1. Oversee construction, printing, and distribution of school's monthly newsletter and review other school publications to public.		
2. Respond promptly and graciously to all correspondance directed to his office.		
3. Frequently provide local papers and radio stations with news releases about Logos School.		
4. Do specific group mailings to grandparents, pastors, donors, etc., with information pertinent and interesting to specified group.		
5. Maintain contact with other Christian development personnel to exchange good ideas.		
6. Regularly inform all parents and patrons of school about scholarships, giving options, etc.		
7. Build, maintain school's mailing list.		

****

SUMMARY COMMENTS:
OBJECTIVES FOR NEXT EVALUATION:
Superintendent's signature: ______________________________
Development Officer's signature: ______________________________
Date: ______________________________

LOGOS SUPERINTENDENT CALENDAR OF TASKS '03–'04

Month	Tasks
JULY	1. Recheck, revise adopted annual budget (enrollments, payroll), inform board 2. Check on progress of textbook, materials purchases 3. Prepare for, complete annual Teacher Training 4. Continue addressing facility needs: maintenance, improvements, new furniture, classroom needs 5. Address any staffing needs, ensure all work agreements are current 6. Receive updated policy manual (check with board clerk) 7. Ensure both yearly calendars are current and sent home 8. Mailing to families/staff to give updates on policies, programs, events 9. Compose, report fiscal year-end figures 10. Ensure board annual report is mailed to parents, etc. 11. Re-issue Materials Contracts for staff authors
AUGUST	1. Compare adopted budget to current payroll, expenses to date, enrollment, needs expected; adjust as necessary 2. Confirm status on all outstanding materials orders 3. Determine any unforeseen classrooms needs (after staff returns) 4. Send Orientation days letter to staff, plan Orientation 5. Determine final enrollment 6. Develop Superintendent goals for the year, copy to principals 7. Ascertain all staff have Work Agreements, other necessary documents 8. Acquaint staff with new/revised policies from board at Orient. 9. Fill any remaining staffing needs 10. Ensure all Teacher Training (ACCS) certificates have been sent, complete any follow-up review of Teacher Training 11. Schedule annual review of financial records/procedures 12. Make daily recess schedule 13. Order faculty service awards (for year-end) 14. Participate in alumni reunion event

SEPTEMBER	1. Verify all financial agreements with families 2. Finalize budget figures, review expenditures for school begin 3. Ensure all preparations are done for the first day of school - facilities, materials, schedules 4. Run first practice fire-drill 5. Send out monthly calendar, after checking with other admin. 6. Participate in first-day assemblies 7. Work on admin.goals for year, get approval by board, assign as appropriate to principals 8. Assign types of funding to build contingency fund (e.g. savings interest, etc.) 9. Set date for school pictures (individual and class) 10. Set time for annual financial review by outside agency 11. Participate in all Back-To-School events 12. Ensure Sub Credit forms are updated 13. Set annual evaluation for curricular review/revision in motion 14. Meet with staff after board meeting
OCTOBER	1. Work on admin goals for year 2. Send out monthly calendar, after checking with other admin. 3. Oversee plans for in-house speech meet 4. Ensure Reformation Day celebrations are appropriate 5. Assist board in preparing for annual meeting 6. Prep for winterizing campus 7. Meet with staff after board meeting
NOVEMBER	1. Send out monthly calendar, after checking with other admin. 2. Ensure all teachers are observed/evaluated this semester 3. Assist in planning/execution of inter-school speech meet 4. Ensure planning of Christmas program is progressing 5. Continue curriculum revision 6. Put together report on school for annual board meeting, after receiving principals' reports 7. Update and mail out Snow Day note to parents, staff phone tree for emergencies 8. Assist with and participate in fundraising evening event 9. Meet with staff after board meeting

DECEMBER	1. Send out monthly calendar, after checking with other admin. 2. Revise form as needed and send survey to staff re: next year's budget 3. Begin preliminary work on next year's budget 4. Participate in Christmas program for elementary 5. Ensure mid-terms and finals are completed on-time 6. Determine facility projects/tasks to be done over break 7. Ensure proper heating settings for buildings over break 8. Organize pizza lunch for staff before break 9. Meet with staff after board meeting
JANUARY	1. After break) Ensure all facility systems are operating well 2. Get budget surveys back in, compile information 3. Make first draft of next year's budget, meet w/other admins to go over, go over w/finance committee 4. Send out monthly calendar 5. Conduct fire drill 6. Present proposed budget to board for first reading and input 7. Order SAT tests for first through eleventh grades 8. Begin planning work for summer Teacher Training 9. Participate in, review quality of Knights' Festival celebration 10. Meet with staff after board meeting
FEBRUARY	1. Send out monthly calendar 2. Submit next year's budget for first reading by board 3. Receive staff retention lists from principals, note possible openings for next year, summit list to board 4. Meet with principals regarding progress on goals 5. Meet with staff after board meeting
MARCH	1. Send out monthly calendar, after checking with other admin 2. Plan for work to be done over spring break 3. Ensure all SAT materials are in 4. Meet with staff after board meeting 5. Participate in Knight Day 6. Prep school for Spring Break, assign any upkeep projects 7. Ensure Teacher Training brochure goes out after spring break 8. Ensure all grades for third quarter go out on time 9. Board adopts version of annual budget

APRIL	1. Send out monthly calendar, after checking with other admin 2. Revised and send out student re-registration forms 3. Construct and send out all new work agreements 4. Estimate classroom seating available 5. Conduct Good Friday assembly 6. Oversee preparations and execution of week of SAT testing 7. Plan and execute annual board visitation day 8. Ensure second semester teacher evaluations are completed 9. Continue advertizing (to parents/churches) staff openings 10. Mail in SAT materials for scoring 11. Meet with staff after board meeting 12. Enquire, arrange for information meetings @ local churches
MAY	1. Send out monthly calendar, after checking with other admin 2. Conduct fire drill 3. Plan and execute year-end staff appreciation dinner 4. Update annual budget as needed 5. Oversee construction of elem and sec annual calendars, submit for board approval 6. Preparations for ACCS conference, select staff to go 7. Ensure plans are in place for HS graduation & eighth grade promotion ceremonies 8. Ensure kindergarten graduation plans are in place 9. Ensure all final report cards are prepared and sent home 10. Distribute year-end program evals. and inventories to staff 11. Ensure all applicable acceptance letters have been mailed 12. Analyze and mail home SAT results with explanation letter 13. Participate in awards assembly and staff recognition events 14. Send home three-month summer calendar 15. Meet with staff after board meeting 16. Research possibility of Summer School program, head
JUNE	1. Determine special summer tasks, assign to staff 2. Ensure summer school plans are set to go, if possible 3. Prepare all necessary teacher training plans with committee 4. Determine and act on any remaining staff positions 5. Determine enrollment and related facility needs 6. Analyze and process all staff year-end evals. of program 7. Ensure revision of curriculum guides are completed, based on year-end teacher input 8. Determine all summer events, schedules in facilities 9. Clear out year's files - keep and apply information as necessary 10. Receive annual board evaluation of superintendent 11. Begin to compile info for board's annual report to constituents 12. Go to ACCS conference (pay per diem to staff going) 13. Evaluate elementary and secondary principals 14. Evaluate Development and Marketing officers

CLASSICAL / CHRISTIAN SCHOOL GROWTH CHART

STAGES OF GROWTH	PHILOSOPHY	BOARD/ ADMINISTRATION	STAFFING	FAMILIES/ STUDENTS	ACADEMIC PROGRAM	OTHER PROGRAMS	FINANCES	FACILITY
Birth - Childhood (0-10 years)	***Adoption of mostly unfamiliar, but very attractive ideas** *Not much time or expertise to determine applications *Borrowed applications (policies) ok	*Usually initial board comprised of a few enthusiastic parents, couples *Little, if any, experience with overseeing school *Long on fervor, short on details of how it will look *Little attention given to board's structure/ purpose *Controversies!	*Board hires young, often single, but excited teachers *Questions on having a principal or not initially *Short-termers for first few years ***Communications between staff and admin/board quickly become an issue for all**	*Initial families composed of first board families *Frequently, disenfranchised families from other Christian schools join *Enthusiasm for start makes for a "honey-moon" period of good will towards all *Quick growth after first year or two	*Adoption of basic classical curriculum from an outside source *Three or four grades offered in some form, typically K-3, some older to coordinate w/ home schooling families *First returns on work very encouraging ***Zealousness can lead to overkill in pacing, level of expectations, homework**	*Easy to fall into many "traditions" in celebrating everything *As older students added, very soon under pressure to add sports,etc. ***Success comes from doing a little as well as possible** *Outside groups want access to the kids constantly	*Good starts set good level of fees to provide good level of salaries, meet overhead needs ***Pressure to constantly do fundraisers of all kinds**	*Churches the obvious and normal choice *Sharing church classrooms often requires some moves on Mondays and Fridays *Used furniture from govn. school auctions *Play areas can become issue
Teens (11-15 years)	***Distinctions from adopted philosophy become evident** *Testing from many trials show up true beliefs *Constant need for articulation of philosophy	*Board matures if longevity present *Smoothing out of" controversial & adversarial meetings—unity should be the norm *Admin/board relations built on two-way trust *Admin. in for long term, if supported	*With maturing of program, staff see career possibilities *More married men and moms in staff *New teachers linked with mentors *Moving past just "doing" curriculum; now helping to design and write ***Teachers earning reputations**	"*Stable core of families to build on *If K-12, first graduates encourage other students, give community good view of school's worth ***School spirit, morale, actual (vs paper) discipline codes apparent** *New families still need convincing	***Early weaknesses addressed; takes real effort to keep pressing for classical application** *Challenges of dialectic and rhetoric levels take much more time to plan *Better base to evaluate and purchase good materials *Often push to make HS program more specific college compatible	*With larger student numbers, drama and sports possible—issues related to quality and student qualifications ***Need for examining philosophy of extra-curricular activities** *Appoint. AD	***Overhead stabilizes, if controlled** *Priority to increase salaries *Possible need for Dev *Decrease in fundraisers	*Outgrowing of first building, expansion or move likely *Planning and funding for new site an excellent time for seeing God's leading ***Anticipate need for compromises, watch debt load**

STAGES OF GROWTH	PHILOSOPHY	BOARD/ ADMINIS-TRATION	STAFFING	FAMILIES/ STUDENTS	ACADEMIC PROGRAM	OTHER PROGRAMS	FINANCES	FACILITY
Adult *(15+ years)*	*Addition of similar, but clarifying documents, books, creeds ***Wider promulgation of philosophy**	*Turn-over of most board members but retention of vision *Policies reviewed annually for applicability *Admin/board working closely to common goals	***Longevity blessings very evident, but difficult to replace veteran staff** *Maturing benefits meet changing needs of staff families	*Earliest families gone, looking toward second generation *Selective appl cation process vs "first-come", looking for good matches *Materials, process to inform of vision ***New "core" develops**	*Constantly reviewing to improve curriculum, teachers' input very valuable *Using more and more home-made materials *Smoother transitions between levels ***Regulated academic requirements**	*Wider recognition, acceptance of programs, positive reviews from others *Increasing desire, ability to produce quality ***Drop some early, burdensome programs**	*Generally stabilized budget, careful growth *Mature development support base *Capital & contingency funds	*Expandable site, additions based on long-range growth plan by board ***Improvements reflect priorities tied to philosophy, not pressures**

www.ingramcontent.com/pod-product-compliance
Lightning Source LLC
LaVergne TN
LVHW020043110826
845155LV00029B/619

* 9 7 8 1 9 4 7 6 4 4 9 3 9 *